HISTORY
of the
HAWAIIAN
KINGDOM

A Revised Edition of
The Hawaiian Monarchy

Norris W. Potter
Lawrence M. Kasdon
Ann Rayson

3565 Harding Avenue
Honolulu, Hawai'i 96816
phone: (808) 734-7159
fax: (808) 732-3627
besspress.com

Design: Carol Colbath
Index: Lee S. Motteler

Cover art, clockwise from upper left corner: Graphic Works; Island Curio; Graphic Works; Kawaiahaʻo Church; Graphic Works; Graphic Works; Graphic Works; Kawaiahaʻo Church

Back cover art: Island Curio

Library of Congress Cataloging-in-Publication Data

Potter, Norris W.
   History of the Hawaiian kingdom /
Norris W. Potter, Lawrence M. Kasdon,
Ann Rayson.
       p.   cm.
   Revised edition of The Hawaiian monarchy,
originally published in 1983.
   Includes illustrations, glossary,
bibliography, index.
   ISBN 1-57306-150-6
1. Hawaii - History. 2. Hawaii -
Kings and Rulers. 3. Hawaii - Politics
and government. I. Kasdon, Lawrence M.
II. Rayson, Ann. III. Title.
DU627.P66 2003   996.9-dc21

Copyright © 2003 by Bess Press, Inc.

Contents

Preface and Acknowledgments

This history of the Hawaiian kingdom, its people, and its government was written by educators in the schools of Hawai'i. The original book by Norris W. Potter and Lawrence M. Kasdon, *Hawaii: Our Island State,* was revised and updated by Ann Rayson, Associate Professor at the University of Hawai'i, to fulfill the need for a textbook specifically covering the historical period from the Western discovery of Hawai'i by Captain James Cook in 1778 to the annexation of Hawai'i by the United States in 1898. This revision, titled *The Hawaiian Monarchy,* has been in print since 1983.

In 2003 *The Hawaiian Monarchy* was revised and rewritten. It is now published as *History of the Hawaiian Kingdom*, with the following new features:

- Reading level reduced by two grades levels: chapters covering unification of the kingdom, contact with Westerners, the Mahele, the influence of the sugar industry, the overthrow of the monarchy, and other topics rewritten for easier readability

- Challenging vocabulary defined in the margins and compiled in a glossary at the end of the text

- Subject matter adapted for a one-semester course

- New color illustrations, including paintings by Herb Kawainui Kāne, never-before-published portraits of monarchs from the Hoffstot Collection at Kawaiaha'o Church, vintage postcards, and "then and now" photographs

- Over two hundred photographs, drawings, and primary source documents from local archives and collections

- A pictorial timeline showing the relationship of events in Hawai'i to those in the United States

- A bibliography of recent related sources, older interpretive writings, and primary sources

- Appendixes covering the formation of the islands, Hawai'i's geography, and Polynesian migration

- New workbook with teacher's answer key as a companion to the new textbook

I wish to thank particularly the people who have made this new *History of the Hawaiian Kingdom* possible: Revé Shapard, editor at Bess Press, who worked to improve and simplify the language while retaining the content of *The Hawaiian Monarchy* in *History of the Hawaiian Kingdom;* Julie Falvey, who obtained artwork, photographs, and primary source documents from various museums, archives, and private collections; Carol Colbath, graphic and book designer, who created the new layout, design, and cover for *History of the Hawaiian Kingdom;* Stephen Foy, M.A. in Hawaiian History, who reviewed *The Hawaiian Monarchy* and gave chapter-by-chapter suggestions for revisions that improve *History of the Hawaiian Kingdom;* all teachers of the history of Hawai'i who answered survey questions and submitted suggestions for this new edition. We appreciate your input, ideas, and continued use of this textbook over the years. We welcome your responses to the new *History of the Hawaiian Kingdom.*

For their generous contributions to the process of obtaining historic artwork and photographs: Herb Kawainui Kāne and Jim Raschick; Woody Kirtley, Graphic Works; Puanani Caindec and the Board of Trustees at Kawaiaha'o Church; Keith Steiner, Island Curio; Marlene Bueltel-Donovan Paahao, Victoria Nihi, Debbe Lee, and Gina Vergara-Bautista, Hawai'i State Archives; Barbara Dunn, Hawaiian Historical Society; Stuart Ching, Mission Houses Museum; Jim Kelly, *The Honolulu Advertiser;* Frank Bridgewater, *Honolulu Star-Bulletin;* DeSoto Brown; Ryan Best, RJBest, Inc.; Lasting Image; Ross Wilson, Current Events; David Gridley, Hawaii Coffee Association; Maia Yannacone.

ANN RAYSON

Soon after the Cook Expedition landed off Kaua'i, a thriving trade developed between the English and the Hawaiians. In this painting, a Hawaiian fisherman holds up fish, offering them for trade. Painting by © Herb Kawainui Kāne

Captain James A. Cook brought Hawai'i and its people to the attention of Europe. Hawai'i State Archives

1
Western Arrival: Captain Cook (1775–1795)

A man and a woman of the Sandwich Islands as drawn by a member of Captain Cook's crew. Hawai'i State Archives

British explorer Captain James A. Cook may not have been the first European to visit the Hawaiian Islands. Some historians claim that a Spanish navigator, Juan Gaetano, visited the Islands in the mid-1500s. However, it was Cook's visits that first brought the Islands to the attention of Europe.

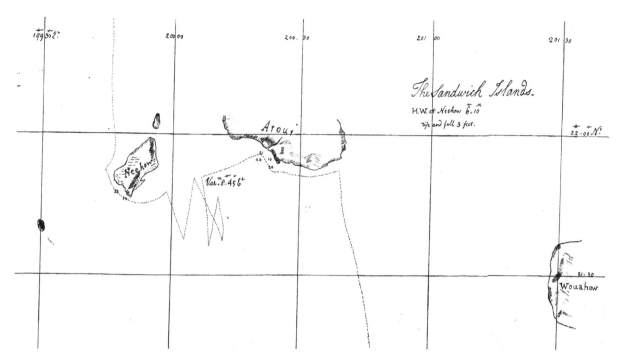

First map of Oʻahu, Kauaʻi, and Niʻihau, drawn by a member of Captain Cook's crew. At the time this map was made, the spellings of the islands were determined by how they were pronounced. Hawaiʻi State Archives

The Voyages of Captain Cook

During his first two voyages Cook explored the southern part of the globe, including New Zealand, the coast of Australia, and some of the Pacific islands. After he completed his first two voyages, many Pacific islands were correctly charted for the first time with the newly invented chronometer. Cook did his work so carefully that since his day there has been little change in the maps of the islands of the southwest Pacific.

In terms of Hawaiian history, Cook's third voyage is most important. On July 12, 1776, Cook set sail on his third voyage with two ships, the *Resolution* and the *Discovery*. He was searching for the Northwest Passage from the Pacific Ocean to the Atlantic Ocean. He sailed around Africa to Tasmania and from there to the Cook Islands and on to Tahiti. Since Cook had visited Tahiti before, he chose it as the place to refit his ships before heading northward to explore the northwest coast of North America. Leaving Tahiti, Cook by chance followed the route taken by the ancient Polynesians who sailed from Tahiti to Hawaiʻi.

chronometer: a very accurate clock that can be used to find longitude

refit: restock and repair

When Captain Cook arrived, the Hawaiians thought he was the god Lono returned. The symbol of Lono was a rectangular banner, and, coincidentally, the sails on Cook's ship were square. In addition, the ships were filled with food, and the Hawaiian legend promised that when Lono returned, he would arrive with food for the people.
Painting by © Herb Kawainui Kāne

First European Visit to the Hawaiian Islands

On January 18, 1778, Cook sighted Oʻahu first and then Kauaʻi. He named the islands the Sandwich Islands in honor of the Earl of Sandwich, who was then the first lord of the British admiralty (a position similar to that of the U.S. secretary of the navy). His first stop in Hawaiʻi was at Waimea, Kauaʻi.

Very soon a thriving trade developed between the English and the Hawaiians. The English needed food, and the Hawaiians wanted the iron nails the English offered in exchange. Although the Hawaiians had small amounts of iron before Cook's arrival (possibly washed ashore from Spanish shipwrecks), it was hard to get, and the Islanders knew its value. They traded sixty pigs, yams, sweet potatoes, cooking bananas, and taro for nails and some pieces of iron.

When Cook went ashore, the people treated him as a

The Hawaiian Islands were originally referred to as the "Sandwich Islands." Captain Cook named the islands after the fourth earl of Sandwich, who was then the first lord of the British admiralty. Hawaiʻi State Archives

thriving: successful

3

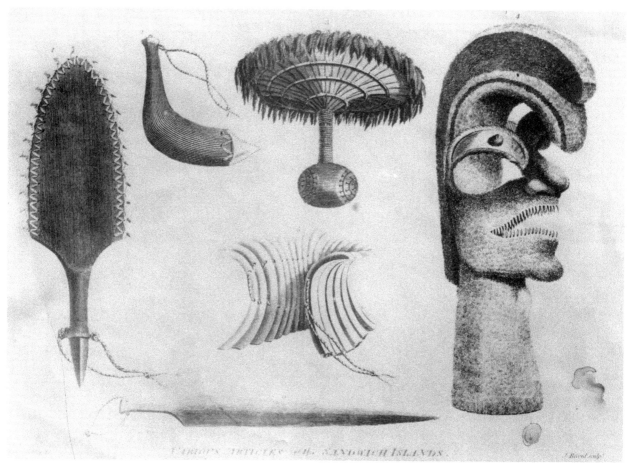

Early Hawaiian warriors used articles such as the wooden *pāhoa*, far left, and the war god Kū, far right, in battle.
Hawai'i State Archives

chief of the highest rank or as a god. The people of Kaua'i may have thought he was the god Lono returned. From Kaua'i Cook sailed to the nearby island of Ni'ihau. He got yams and salt there. In return he gave the people of Ni'ihau goats and pigs, as well as melon, pumpkin, and onion seeds. After two weeks, Cook sailed off to explore the northwestern part of the North American coastline.

Late in the fall Cook and his crews returned to Hawai'i to spend the winter and explore the islands more thoroughly. After charting the coasts of Maui and Hawai'i, Cook anchored at Kealakekua Bay on the Kona coast of the island of Hawai'i to refit his ships. The Hawaiians were quite excited by the sight of Cook's ships as he explored the two islands. This visit, as well as his first one, occurred in the Makahiki season, sacred to the peaceful god Lono. Maybe the *kāhuna* believed that Cook's return fulfilled the legend of the god

kāhuna: priests, experts

4

The Cook Expedition entered Kealakekua Bay in January 1779. Painting by © Herb Kawainui Kāne

Lono. According to Hawaiian legend, Lono had sailed away promising to return someday. The Englishmen fitted the description of Lono, and even the sails on their ships were square, like one of the symbols sacred to Lono. As promised in the legend, the ships were full of food.

While the two ships were being repaired, the English traded with the Hawaiians. The king, Kalaniʻōpuʻu, visited Cook aboard the *Resolution* and exchanged gifts with him. The king gave Cook several feather cloaks and some food. Cook gave the king a linen shirt and a sword. Later Cook presented the king with a tool chest.

Much of the iron traded was in the form of daggers, made by the ship's blacksmiths. These were modeled after the Hawaiians' wooden *pāhoa*. There were no serious quarrels between the English and the Hawaiians. Nothing suggested the tragic events to follow.

daggers: short, pointed weapons with sharp edges

pāhoa: Hawaiian dagger

The Death of Cook

In eighteen days the repairs were completed, and the ships were loaded with supplies. Cook left Kealakekua,

On February 14, 1779, Cook's crew returned to Kealakekua Bay unannounced to repair their ship. Fighting broke out between the Hawaiians and Captain Cook and his crew, and Captain Cook was killed in the brawl.

Painting by © Herb Kawainui Kāne

planning to return to the Pacific Northwest. However, a few days later a storm damaged the *Resolution* and forced him to return to Kealakekua Bay.

This time Cook was not received so happily. The season of Kū, a war god, had begun. Supplying food for the crew of the two ships had left the Hawaiians with barely enough food for themselves. They quarreled with Cook's crew, threw rocks at some crew members who had gone ashore, and stole a large ship's boat and broke it up to get the nails.

Cook took command of a group going ashore to recover the boat. He planned to lure the king onboard ship and hold him hostage until the boat was returned. Cook almost succeeded, but trouble broke out as he was returning with the king. During the fighting Cook was killed.

The Hawaiians carried away the bodies of Cook and four sailors who had also been killed in the fight. Cook's body was treated like that of a high chief or a god. As was the custom, the flesh was removed and some of the bones distributed among the high chiefs. Captain Clerke, now commander of the expedition, and most of the Hawaiian leaders favored a peaceful settlement. Nevertheless, some fighting continued until parts of Cook's body were returned. The Hawaiians showed great courage against the superior weapons of the English.

A monument to Cook stands today at Kealakekua Bay.

Captain George Vancouver

As a result of Cook's voyages, the fur trade developed in the Pacific Northwest at the end of the eighteenth century. Hawai'i became a favorite wintering place for fur traders and traders in general. Four years after Cook made his last voyage, ships began to call at the Islands. The French explorer La Perouse came to the Islands, as did British and Spanish explorers. Of those early visitors, however, Captain George Vancouver stands out.

Vancouver had visited the Islands in 1778 and 1779 as a junior officer under Cook. In 1791 England sent him to the Pacific to receive certain lands on the northwest coast of North America from Spain. He was also to complete the exploration of the coast that was begun by Cook. Then he

The Cook Monument marks the place of Captain Cook's death at Kealakekua Bay, Hawai'i. Hawai'i State Archives

Vancouver and Kamehameha sailed together on the *Discovery* from Hilo to Kealakekua Bay in January 1794.
Painting by © Herb Kawainui Kāne

7

Kamehameha I befriended George Vancouver and considered him one of his closest advisers. Vancouver brought cattle, sheep, goats, and geese as gifts to the Hawaiians and advised Kamehameha on organizing his troops. Hawai'i State Archives

kapu: something that is not allowed

man-of-war: warship

was to make a survey of the Hawaiian Islands and spend the winter there.

Vancouver brought cattle, sheep, goats, and geese as gifts to the Hawaiians. Kamehameha (whose role in Hawaiian history is described in chapters 2 and 3) realized the importance of conservation. He placed a ten-year *kapu* on the cattle so that they would have a chance to multiply. Vancouver also gave the chiefs of the different islands grapevines, orange and almond trees, and garden seeds.

Vancouver's gifts supplied the traders with beef and added variety to the Hawaiians' diet. His most important contribution, however, was promoting peace among the warring chiefs. He spent much time advising Kamehameha on ruling his kingdom and dealing with foreigners. Unlike most foreigners visiting the Islands during this period, he refused to supply guns to any of the chiefs in Hawai'i, but he did help strengthen the position of the king in other ways. Vancouver's carpenters helped build the first European-type vessel in the Hawaiian Islands and promised the king a British man-of-war, which was sent some years later. Vancouver also taught the king how to drill his troops.

Because of Vancouver's influence, Kamehameha offered to place his kingdom under the protection of Great Britain. The British government did not act upon this offer.

Summing Up the Chapter

Although Captain Cook made three voyages to the Pacific, it was not until the third voyage that he visited the Hawaiian Islands. Because of the conditions surrounding his visit, Hawaiians may have thought he was the god Lono. A thriving trade began between the English and the Hawaiians. Later, trouble broke out over the theft of a boat, and Cook was killed in the fighting that followed. As adviser to King Kamehameha, the English Captain Vancouver helped bring peace within the Islands, at the same time making the king's position stronger.

2
King Kamehameha I
(1795–1819)

TAMEHAMEHA

Kamehameha I was a strong warrior and a great leader. As a child, he battled his brother Kīwala'ō for control of the throne and succeeded. As king, he united the Hawaiian Islands and formed friendships with westerners that would later bring social, religious, and commercial change to the Islands. Kamehameha's name was spelled "Tamehameha" before "T" became "K" when the Hawaiian alphabet was standardized. Painting by © Herb Kawainui Kāne

Kamehameha was born at Kohala, on the northern side of the island of Hawai'i, sometime between 1753 and 1760. His parents were the chief Keōua and the chiefess Keku'iapoiwa. Some accounts say that Kahekili, later the king of Maui, was the natural father.

Kamehameha's Early Life

Keku'iapoiwa's uncle, Alapa'inui, the ruling chief of the island, believed that Kamehameha would grow up to be a threat to him. Knowing that her uncle wanted to kill the baby, Keku'iapoiwa hid him with the chief Nae'ole. Nae'ole and Keku'iapoiwa's cousin Kaha'ōpulani became his foster parents. They called him Pai'ea. When Pai'ea was five years old, he returned to live with his parents. Alapa'inui, who no longer considered the boy to be a threat, named him Kamehameha.

When Kamehameha was about twelve, he was taken to the court of his uncle Kalani'ōpu'u, the ruling chief of Hawai'i. There he received training for battle from the famous warrior Kekūhaupi'o.

Shortly after the arrival of Captain Cook an event occurred that was a turning point in Kamehameha's life. In 1780 Kalani'ōpu'u, perhaps sensing that he had not long to live, called a meeting of high-ranking chiefs. He announced that his successor was to be his son Kīwala'ō. His younger son, Keōua Kūahu'ula, was to receive land. Kamehameha was to take care of Kūkā'ilimoku, the family war god.

A bitter rivalry developed between Kīwala'ō and Kamehameha. One event in particular angered Kīwala'ō. A rebel chief was captured and brought to a *heiau* in the Ka'ū district to be sacrificed to the war god. He was clubbed or stabbed to death, and his body was laid upon the altar. Kīwala'ō, representing the king, was supposed to offer the sacrifice, but suddenly Kamehameha stepped forward and offered the sacrifice himself. Perhaps powerful friends urged him to take this bold step. Perhaps he believed that as caretaker of the war god he should take the central role in the sacrifice. As a result, Kalani'ōpu'u advised him to leave. This he did, taking with him a group of supporters and the war god.

successor: the person who follows after or replaces another in an office or position, such as king

Kūkā'ilimoku: one of the forms of the god Kū; Kamehameha's family war god

rivalry: competition

heiau: temple

Kamehameha requested that special war canoes be built for his conquest of the islands. Painting by © Herb Kawainui Kāne

Early in 1782 Kalani'ōpu'u died. Two rival groups of chiefs were formed. Each looked out for its own interests. On one side were the chiefs of Kona, who had persuaded Kamehameha to join them. On the other side were the young king, Kīwala'ō, his uncle, Keawema'uhili, and his half-brother Keōua.

Within a few months the two sides were at war. The climax of the struggle took place at Moku'ōhai in the summer of 1782. Kamehameha's forces won, and Kīwala'ō was killed. The surviving chiefs seized different areas of the island. Keōua took Ka'ū and part of Puna. His uncle took Hilo and adjoining areas in Puna and Hāmākua. Kamehameha took Kona, his own Kohala, and northern Hāmākua.

The "Law of The Splintered Paddle"

For the next nine years the history of Hawai'i is one of civil war. The long struggle finally ended with the victory of

civil war: fighting between groups or regions within the same country

unification: bringing together into one unit

Kamehameha over Keōua, Keawemaʻuhili, and Kahekili, and with the unification of the Islands. Out of this period came a number of stories. Abraham Fornander in his classic history of Hawaiʻi tells this tale:

> Kamehameha started one day with his own war canoe and its crew alone, without making his object known to his counselors, and unaccompanied by any of them. Steering for the Puna coast, he ran in upon the reef at a place called Papai in Keaau. A number of fishermen with their wives and children were out fishing on the reef, and, as they were about returning ashore, Kamehameha rushed upon them with the object of slaying or capturing as many as he could, they being the subjects of Keawemauhili. The greater number of these people saved themselves by flight, but two men were hemmed off and they engaged in fight with Kamehameha. During the scuffle Kamehameha's foot slipped into a crevice of the coral reef, and, while thus entangled, he was struck some severe blows on the head with the fisherman's paddle. Luckily for Kamehameha the fisherman was encumbered with a child on his back, and ignorant of the real name and character of his antagonist. Extricating himself with a violent effort, Kamehameha reached his canoe and returned to Laupahoehoe.

encumbered: held back; slowed down

antagonist: opponent, enemy

extricating: freeing

Kamehameha realized that his narrow escape from death was a result of his own attack on peaceful people. Twelve years later, in 1797, he created a law punishing robbery and murder with death. He called the law *māmalahoe*, or "splintered paddle."

māmalahoe: splintered paddle

The Death of Keōua

Another tale tells of the misfortunes of Keōua. After a battle with Kamehameha's forces, he had retreated through Hilo on his way home to Kaʻū. On this return march, Kīlauea volcano erupted suddenly during the night, terrifying Keōua's forces camped nearby. They tried to appease Pele, goddess of the volcano, by rolling stones into the crater. But more eruptions came on the second and third nights. On the third day, Keōua ordered his army to set forth in three different companies. The lead company had not gone far when a new explosion sent clouds of hot cinders into the air. A few men were burned or suffocated to death by falling cinders. The rear group, which was not badly harmed, pressed forward to escape the danger. Most of the deadly ashes fell upon the middle group.

In Ka'ū the following year, 1791, two advisers of Kamehameha urged Keōua to meet their leader at a large new *heiau* built in honor of Kamehameha's war god at Pu'ukoholā. Here, they said, peace would be restored between the two warriors and the disastrous civil war ended.

Although he was suspicious, Keōua agreed to the meeting. He gathered some of his followers in a fleet of canoes for the journey to Kawaihae. When the canoes approached

Kīlauea Volcano began to erupt while Keōua's forces were nearby. Island Curio

appease: to calm

disastrous: terrible; causing great destruction and unhappiness

Thousands of men helped build Pu'ukoholā Heiau near Kawaihae, Kohala, on Hawai'i. Painting by © Herb Kawainui Kāne

Keōua agreed to meet Kamehameha at the heiau. When Keōua arrived, he was killed by one of Kamehameha's warriors. Painting by © Herb Kawainui Kāne

slaughter: the killing of a large number of people

the shore, he saw a crowd of armed warriors and chiefs surrounding Kamehameha, who stood on the beach. As he was leaving his canoe, Keōua was killed by a spear in the hands of Keʻeaumoku, one of Kamehameha's warriors. All in Keōua's canoe were also killed. Finally, Kamehameha stopped the slaughter. The body of Keōua was sacrificed to the war god at the *heiau*.

It is not clear whether Kamehameha was directly responsible for the killings. He may have been following the rough code of his day. Perhaps he could not safely resist the will of some of his powerful supporters. Or perhaps he wanted to end the bitter rivalries that were wasting the land. In any case, the island of Hawaiʻi was now firmly in his hands. He could proceed with his plans to conquer the other islands.

Kamehameha was successful not only because he was a strong leader but also because he made good use of the weapons and skills of foreigners who joined his forces. The most important of these were John Young, the English boatswain on the American ship *Eleanora*, and Isaac Davis, a sailor on the *Fair American*. After a series of colorful adventures, these two men became advisers to Kamehameha.

Civil War in the Islands

The chief obstacle in Kamehameha's path of conquest was Kahekili, who had won control of the islands of Maui, Lānaʻi, Molokaʻi, and Oʻahu. Through his brother Kāʻeo, Kahekili also controlled Kauaʻi.

Suddenly, as though to show that the gods favored Kamehameha, came the news of the death of Kahekili. His lands were to be divided between his brother Kāʻeo and his son Kalanikūpule.

Then, as if another sign from the gods, Kāʻeo and

The body of Keōua was sacrificed to the war god during a special ceremony at Puʻukoholā Heiau.
Painting by © Herb Kawainui Kāne

boatswain: a low-ranking ship's officer in change of the rigging, anchors, cables, and deck crew

John Young and Isaac Davis helped Kamehameha conquer and unite the islands. In this painting, Kamehameha talks with Young and Davis aboard the *Fair American*. Painting by © Herb Kawainui Kāne

skirmish: a small or less important
    battle

mutiny: open rebellion against a
    leader by his followers

plunder: to rob, especially during a
    war

provisioned: stocked with food and
    other supplies

artillerymen: soldiers trained in the
    use of weapons

Kalanikūpule quarreled. The first skirmish between Kā'eo and the warriors of Kalanikūpule took place at Waimānalo on O'ahu in the summer of 1794. It was ended by the arrival of Kalanikūpule, and peace was restored. Kā'eo soon learned of a plot against him organized by his own followers. To put down this mutiny, he formed a plan to turn upon Kalanikūpule and plunder the lands he ruled.

In November 1794, Kā'eo started overland from Wai'anae through the 'Ewa district to 'Aiea, near Pearl Harbor. At first he was successful. The tide of battle was turned when three trading vessels entered Pearl Harbor. One was commanded by English Captain William Brown, the other by American Captain John Kendrick. Kalanikūpule asked for help from Brown, who gave him guns and boats manned by a small group of sailors. The main action took place on December 12. Kā'eo's forces retreated in the face of fire from the boats. Kā'eo and a few followers fought bravely but were finally killed.

Kalanikūpule and his chiefs then plotted to seize the two English ships, kill the captains, and use the ships to attack Kamehameha himself.

While the ship's boats, returning with a load of salt, were grounded by the low water on the reef at Ke'ehi, Kalanikūpule's men attacked the remaining crews of the two ships. They killed the captains and forced the crewmen to make ready for the sea. As they were ready to sail, however, the English crews regained control of the ships. They killed or drove off the attackers and raced for Hawai'i. There they provisioned their ships, left word for Kamehameha about the events on O'ahu, and continued on their way to China.

The Battle of Nu'uanu

Kamehameha knew it was time to try to take control of all the islands. Swiftly he gathered a great fleet of canoes, thousands of warriors, and a group of foreign artillerymen headed by Isaac Davis and John Young. The time was February 1795.

He attacked first Maui, then Moloka'i. For the attack on O'ahu, the long line of canoes extended along the shore from the present Wai'alae Golf Course to Waikīkī. Here Kamehameha grouped his forces for the attack on

Kalanikūpule, who had taken positions in Nuʻuanu Valley. Adding strength to Kalanikūpule's army were the chief Kaʻiana, his brother Nahiolea, and their close friends and followers. They had all deserted Kamehameha after the voyage from Hawaiʻi had begun.

The battle of Nuʻuanu, in April 1795, is one of the greatest stories in Hawaiʻi's history. The beautiful valley, once filled with the shouts of warriors, is now a favorite spot of visitors and residents. The outcome of the battle, according to Fornander, was as follows:

> At Puiwa the hostile forces met, and for a while the victory was hotly contested; but the superiority of Kamehameha's artillery, the number of his guns, and the better practice of his soldiers soon turned the day in his favor . . . . Of [the Oʻahu forces] who were not killed, some escaped up the sides of the mountains that enclose the valley on either side, while a large number were driven over the pali of Nuʻuanu, . . . several hundred feet in height, and perished miserably. Kaiana and his brother Nahiolea were killed early in the battle. Kaolaukani, the brother of Kalanikupule, escaped to Kauai. Kalanikupule was hotly pursued, but he escaped in the jungle, and for several months . . . [lived] in the mountain-range that separates Koolaupoko from Ewa, until finally he was captured in the upper portion of Waipio, killed, brought to Kamehameha, and sacrificed to the war god Kukailimoku.

A warrior of old Hawaiʻi
Painting by © Herb Kawainui Kāne

The battle of Nuʻuanu was a turning point in Hawaiian history, but it did not lead immediately to the firm unification of the islands. Revolts broke out from time to time, and the island of Kauaʻi was still independent. However, it was only a matter of time until Kamehameha would become the single ruler of the whole island chain.

Although the bitter wars among the chiefs had now come to an end, a new influence was at work in the Islands

The battle of Nu'uanu was the last battle fought to secure Kamehameha's position as the single ruler of the islands. In battle, hundreds of warriors were killed, many of them driven over the steep edge of the *pali* (cliff).

Painting by © Herb Kawainui Kāne

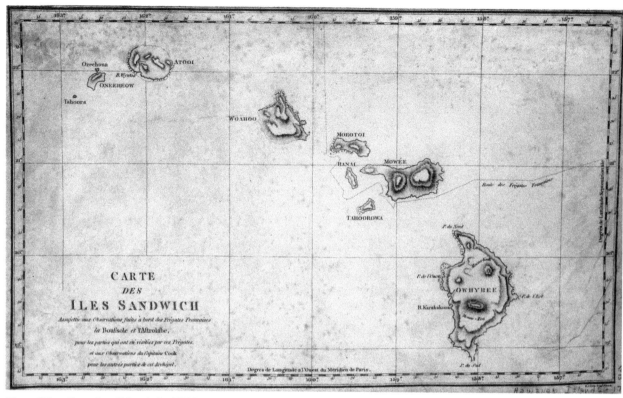

Map of the Hawaiian Islands in 1798. Hawai'i State Archives

haole: foreigners

that would change Hawaiian life and customs. Increasingly during the civil wars, *haole* from many countries had visited or moved to the Islands. The changes they brought during the last years of Kamehameha's reign are described in the next chapter.

Summing Up the Chapter

Kamehameha I was born at Kohala some time between 1753 and 1760. Having been given custody of the war god by King Kalani'ōpu'u, Kamehameha became a bitter rival of the king's son, Kīwala'ō, for control of Hawai'i. In the wars that followed, Kamehameha's forces were victorious. The victory on the Big Island was followed by victories over Keōua, Keawema'uhili, Kahekili, and Kalanikūpule and the final unification of the chain of islands under the leadership of Kamehameha. Kamehameha combined his own skills and qualities of leadership with the help of weapons and men furnished by the foreigners, who were coming to the Islands in greater numbers.

King Kamehameha Statue

Today in downtown Honolulu stands a much-photographed statue of Kamehameha. On June 11 it is draped with flower *lei* in his honor. The public holiday was first proclaimed in 1871 by Kamehameha V "in memory of our Grandfather and Predecessor, Kamehameha I, the founder of the Hawaiian Kingdom." The bronze figure is larger than life-size, and the features are not a true likeness. When the legislature of the kingdom set aside funds for the statue in 1878, King Kalākaua chose the handsomest man in the court as a model. This statue, done by an American sculptor living in Florence, Italy, was lost when the ship bringing it to Hawai'i sank. The legislature collected $10,000 insurance and ordered another statue, which now stands near 'Iolani Palace. The original statue was salvaged, then shipped to Kohala on the island of Hawai'i, the birthplace of Kamehameha.

salvaged: rescued, saved.

The Kamehameha statue on King Street honors the memory of King Kamehameha I. On King Kamehameha Day, the statue is draped with leis.
Wikipedia

B. Bess

3
The Old Order Changes (1815-1825)

During the last years of his life, Kamehameha acted as an administrator. He organized a system of government, enforced the *kapu*, and encouraged trade with foreigners. Painting by © Herb Kawainui Kāne

After the battle of Nuʻuanu, Kamehameha's great task was to unite and improve his new kingdom. He based his government largely on the old Hawaiian land system. He rewarded his main chiefs with grants of land. They collected taxes in the traditional way, receiving food and other gifts from the commoners.

In 1796 Kamehameha gathered his canoes at Waiʻanae and set forth to conquer Kauaʻi. In midchannel a great storm sank many of his canoes and forced him to give up the attempt. Several months later, he quickly smashed a revolt that broke out on the island of Hawaiʻi.

This was Kamehameha's last important military action. Now he was free to take on his new role as an administrator. He kept some of the more restless chiefs near his court. He made others, whom he trusted completely, governors of the various islands. John Young became governor of the island of Hawaiʻi. Keʻeaumoku became governor of Maui. At court, Kamehameha depended greatly on the powerful Kona chiefs and their sons and on Kalanimōkū, "the iron cable of Hawaiʻi." Kalanimōkū's ability led admiring English sailors to name him after their own prime minister, William Pitt. They called Kalanimōkū "Billy Pitt."

The king strictly enforced the *kapu* system, believing that it strengthened his control. One of his first projects was to rebuild his war-torn land. He set his people to work terracing hills, banking up taro patches, digging long irrigation ditches, and building fishponds. The king himself took an active part in these public works. Captain Archibald Campbell, in his description of Hawaiʻi about 1810, mentions seeing Kamehameha deep in the mud of a taro patch:

> This mode of culture is particularly laborious, and in all the operations those engaged are almost constantly up to the middle in mud. . . . I have often seen the king working hard in a taro patch. I know not whether this was done with a view of setting an example of industry to his subjects. Such exertion could scarcely be thought necessary among these islanders who are certainly the most industrious people I ever saw.

traditional: passed down from generation to generation

commoners: the people who did not have the rank of chiefs; in Hawaiʻi they were known as the *makaʻāinana*

administrator: someone who manages people and events

kapu system: a set of rules telling Hawaiians what they could and could not do

166 Taro, Hawaiians make Poi from this Plant, Hawaiian Islands.

Taro was an important crop to the Hawaiians. After the war, the Hawaiians banked taro patches to rebuild war-torn lands. Island Curio

Indians in the Pacific Northwest sold furs to British and American traders. Up to 1791, nearly all the ships arriving in Hawai'i were those of British fur traders. Painting by © Herb Kawainui Kāne

The Fur Trade

During Kamehameha's reign, trade with foreigners increased greatly. When Captain Cook's journals were published in 1784, the world learned of the wealth of China and of the Pacific Northwest, which included present-day Washington, Oregon, and British Columbia. British traders exploited the fur resources, using the furs to pay for tea and other goods purchased in China. Up to 1791 nearly all the ships arriving in Hawai'i were those of British fur traders.

Soon after gaining independence, Americans entered the Pacific fur trade. By 1810 they controlled most of the fur trade between the northwest coast and Canton, China.

After the Revolutionary War, Americans were cut off from their normal markets in the British Empire and had little silver or few goods to trade. They wanted the tea, cotton cloth,

exploited: made use of selfishly

and silk of China, but they needed something they could give the Chinese merchants in return. The Chinese were willing to pay well for furs. This led the Americans to enter the fur trade in competition with traders of several nations.

Soon after the fur trade began, ships began to stop at the Hawaiian Islands, for many reasons. First, supplies in the amounts needed for ships were not available along the West Coast. Second, captains needed men for their ships, and Hawaiians were excellent seamen. Third, fresh fruits and vegetables, available in the Islands, were necessary to prevent scurvy. Fourth, the Islands offered a convenient place to refit ships. Fifth, after 1805, few ships were able to complete their trading in one summer because of the increasing scarcity of furs and sea otter skins. Sailors were more willing to sign on for the longer journeys if they knew the ship would winter in the Sandwich Islands.

scurvy: a disease caused by lack of vitamin C

scarcity: shortage

In the early 1800s, ships from all over the world visited the Sandwich Islands. Kamehameha carefully monitored the traffic in the bay from a small guardhouse in the distance. John Young, a close adviser to Kamehameha, is pictured in the foreground, at the far right. Painting by © Herb Kawainui Kāne

In the early 1800s most of the ships that stopped in the Islands carrying furs were American. These early traders obtained food, water, firewood, and salt for curing hides. In the early days of the fur trade, islanders were eager to exchange their goods for a few scraps of iron and nails. Before the Islands were united, their chiefs got arms and ammunition in exchange for their goods. After the unification, cloth became the main item of exchange. The islanders quickly became skillful at bargaining and steadily raised their prices. The Russian world traveler Lisianski wrote that a small pig cost him an iron ax. A hundred pounds of sweet potatoes cost three yards of linen, while a small knife was the price of a fowl.

Originally, the ships traveled around Cape Horn and into the Pacific, going either directly to the Islands or first to the northwest. After a while the traders learned that they could earn high profits by carrying on smuggling operations with the Spanish settlements in California and Mexico. At times they supplied the Russian outposts in Alaska and Kamchatka (Russia), taking fur in exchange. By 1812 they added sandalwood from the Hawaiian and Marquesas Islands to their cargoes of furs. After the Spanish colonies on the Pacific coast became independent, the Americans traded with them.

The Sandalwood Trade

No one knows for sure how traders found out about Hawaiian sandalwood, which has a natural pleasant smell in the wood. Sticks of sandalwood may have been in a load of firewood brought to an American ship. By 1790, sea captains were sending crewmen to search for sandalwood. By 1805 it had become an important export item. The peak of the trade was reached in 1818. Most of the trading was with Americans, but sandalwood's main market was China.

Seeing its value, Kamehameha declared the sandalwood trade a royal monopoly. The chiefs traded in the name of the king. The king himself became a skilled bargainer. If he was unsure of a trade, he would not complete it without consulting one of his advisers, such as John Young.

Travelers to the Islands reported that whole villages were deserted while the people were in the mountains cutting

Travelers to the Islands reported that whole villages were deserted while people were in the mountains cutting sandalwood.
Hawai'i State Archives

sandalwood. The Hawaiians owned few horses; therefore, the islanders themselves carried the sandalwood many miles. This labor weakened the workers and left them little time to cultivate their fields. When the king learned of this condition, he ordered the chiefs and commoners not to spend all their time cutting sandalwood. He placed a *kapu* on young trees in order to conserve this natural resource.

Kamehameha wanted to build up a fleet of ships, for both trade and military purposes. Before he died he had bought at least six ships. Two months before he died, Kamehameha bought sixteen kegs of rum, a box of tea, and eight thousand dollars worth of guns and ammunition, paying for them with sandalwood.

Near the end of his reign, Kamehameha tried to enter

A list of goods received by King Kamemeha in exchange for a shipload of sandalwood

3 paintings on paper

1 box of Chinese wood

3 dozen ordinary cotton stockings

2 crystal lamps

1 bundle of metal pipes

6 boxes

1 bundle of bluestones and white
    for a gaming table

1000 large beads

10 boxes of silk handkerchiefs

6 shiny hats for soldiers

12 black straw hats

50 silk hats

6 reels of thread

3 pieces of flowered flannel

6 fishing rods

100 Chinese mats

135 lbs. large glass beads

1 saddle

3 pieces flowered satin

3 boxes of sweets

1 large cloak

bartered: traded

promissory notes: written promises
    to repay a certain amount at a
    certain time

picul: a measure used for sandal-
    wood. One picul equaled 133.5
    pounds and was worth about 8 or
    10 dollars.

into the overseas sandalwood trade. He sent a ship loaded with sandalwood to Canton. The sandalwood could not be sold at a profit, and port charges added to the expense of the voyage. Kamehameha learned that other nations charged visiting ships for harbor, pilot, and port fees. He decided to do the same at the harbor in Honolulu.

Sandalwood was usually bartered for goods. In the early years of trade, Hawaiians were offered simple items such as bits of metal scraps and nails. By the 1820s, however, they wanted different types of goods. They wanted blankets, cotton, silks, turpentine, hardwood, muskets and powder, alcohol, and rice. A few years later, they added goods made in England to the list.

After Kamehameha died, all royal controls on the sandalwood trade, which had become the main source of the Islands' wealth, were ended. Liholiho, who succeeded his father as Kamehameha II, allowed favorite chiefs to engage in the trade. In the following years, competing traders tried to persuade chiefs to sell sandalwood for goods for which they had little need.

The traders were so eager to sell their goods that they let the chiefs buy on credit. Since the chiefs could not always deliver the sandalwood immediately, they signed promissory notes to pay a certain number of piculs of the wood. Often the notes could not be collected. If the traders pressed too hard for payment, the chiefs would buy fewer goods. The chiefs were also reluctant to pay when they found, for example, that ships were rotten. Meanwhile, the supply of sandalwood became scarcer each year.

Results of the Fur and Sandalwood Trade

Before the arrival of Captain Cook, the Hawaiians produced nearly everything they needed and only as much as they could use. The fur and sandalwood trade led to the introduction of new goods from Europe, the United States, and China. The Hawaiian economy was now one of trade and gain.

At first, only the king and the chiefs benefited from this trade. Even under the royal monopoly, the chiefs kept four-tenths of the sandalwood they collected for private trading. The royal monopoly ended with the death of Kamehameha I.

Before the arrival of Captain Cook, Hawaiians produced nearly everything they needed and only as much as they could use. Painting by © Herb Kawainui Kāne

Some imported *haole* goods were American cottons, woolens, nails, English saddles, Russian canvas, Guayaquil cocoa, flour, soap, rice, hemp, French wines, Manila cordage, Chinese cotton cloth, turpentine, crockery and glass, harnesses, iron pots and pans, papers, and ink. Very little money was used up to 1825, as most of the imports were traded for food or sandalwood.

New foods were added to the native diet. By 1825 cabbage, potatoes, corn, limes, and pineapple appeared in the markets of Honolulu. Ducks, turkeys, and European breeds of chickens, pigs, and dogs were also introduced. Mango trees were brought to Hawai'i in 1824.

Another result of the fur and sandalwood trade was the settlement of foreigners in the Islands. Some worked for the kings and chiefs. They built sloops and schooners for inter-island trade, transported provisions, and gathered sandalwood. Others were businessmen, ranchers, or missionaries. But most of the foreign residents were drifters and stranded or runaway sailors.

Guayaquil: a city in western Ecuador

Manila: a city in the Philippine Islands

crockery: pottery made from clay fired at fairly low temperatures

sloop: a sailing boat with a single mast

schooner: a sailing vessel with at least two masts; the largest sail is on the aftermost mast

Schooners carried goods for interisland trade. Painting by © Herb Kawainui Kāne

immunity: protection or resistance

The coming of foreigners had a terrible effect on islanders' health. The common diseases of foreigners, such as measles, influenza, and colds, to which the Hawaiians had no natural immunity, were fatal to large numbers. Also, heavy drinking of alcohol, introduced by the foreigners, weakened the health of Hawaiians.

Kauaʻi and Niʻihau

Although storm and disease had broken up his first two attempts to conquer Kauaʻi, Kamehameha did not give up. In 1810 Kaumualiʻi, the ruler of Kauaʻi and Niʻihau, realized that his army could not long resist the military force that was building up on Oʻahu and that it would be better to surrender. Through a friendly American trader named

Captain Nathan Winship, he arranged to meet Kamehameha. Taking passage on Winship's vessel, he journeyed to O'ahu. Kamehameha received him generously and honorably. In return for the surrender of the islands, he was allowed to remain as their governor as long as he lived. After he died the position would go to the Kamehameha line.

Meanwhile, some of Kamehameha's chiefs plotted to poison Kaumuali'i, who had held out against Kamehameha for so many years. Isaac Davis learned of the plot and persuaded Captain Winship to take Kaumuali'i back to Kaua'i on short notice. The chiefs, angry at Davis's interference, poisoned him, ending the life of one of Kamehameha's most loyal servants.

The Russians Come to Hawai'i

During the last years of Kamehameha's reign, foreign ships, mostly British and American, were familiar sights along the Honolulu waterfront. In 1804, and again in 1809, vessels flying the Russian flag made brief visits to the Islands.

Some years earlier, the Russian government had given a monopoly of the fur trade in the north Pacific to the Russian American Company. In 1812 the Russians founded a settlement at Fort Ross, on the California coast north of San Francisco, and one in Sitka, Alaska. To supply these settlements, the governor of the Russian company, Alexander Baranoff, sent a ship to Hawai'i in 1814 to pick up cargo. After loading, the ship set sail in January of 1815 but was wrecked on the shore at Waimea, Kaua'i.

Baranoff then sent a German doctor named Georg Scheffer to recover the cargo and possibly set up a permanent trading post in the Islands. Scheffer paid his respects to Kamehameha on the Big Island and then proceeded to Kaua'i on a ship that Baranoff had sent to him. Here he wormed his way into Kaumuali'i's confidence, and in the spring of 1816 started trading operations. Apparently he also succeeded in involving Kaumuali'i in a treasonable agreement to make the island a protectorate of the Russian czar.

Scheffer then returned to Honolulu. With a force from three Russian vessels anchored in the harbor he built a blockhouse, mounted guns, and raised the Russian flag.

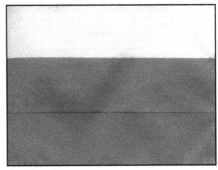
Russian flag

treasonable: disloyal

protectorate: a country or region under the protection and partial control of a stronger country

The Honolulu Fort was built to protect Honolulu from foreign invasions. Hawai'i State Archives

Fort Street Mall was named after the Honolulu Fort. B. Bess

This daring action was reported to Kamehameha, who sent word to his chiefs on O'ahu to oppose the invaders. Faced with superior force, the Russians withdrew to Kaua'i. Kamehameha promptly ordered John Young to build a strong fort that included the Russian blockhouse. Young mounted sixty guns on it and placed others on the slopes of Punchbowl Hill overlooking the town. Fort Street in today's downtown Honolulu takes its name from this incident.

By this time American traders had convinced Kaumuali'i that this Russian influence was dangerous. When orders came from Kamehameha to expel Scheffer, Kaumuali'i agreed to follow them. Scheffer left suddenly for Canton and finally reached St. Petersburg, in Russia.

When the Russian imperial navy ship *Rurick* visited the islands in late 1816, its commanding officer, Lieutenant Otto von Kotzebue, showed his approval of Kamehameha's action in expelling Scheffer and stated that his government had only the friendliest of feelings for Hawai'i.

The Last Days of Kamehameha

In 1811 Kamehameha set forth on a tour of his kingdom, starting with the island of Hawai'i. On the way, however, his schooner *Keōua* sprang a leak and had to return to Honolulu. From there Captain Winship took the king on his ship to Kealakekua Bay, where Kamehameha stayed for a short time. He then visited Maui and Moloka'i, where he organized the system of collecting taxes and inspired his subjects to improve their farming methods.

Queen Keōpūolani bore Kamehameha two more children. (Their first child, Liholiho, who would become Kamehameha

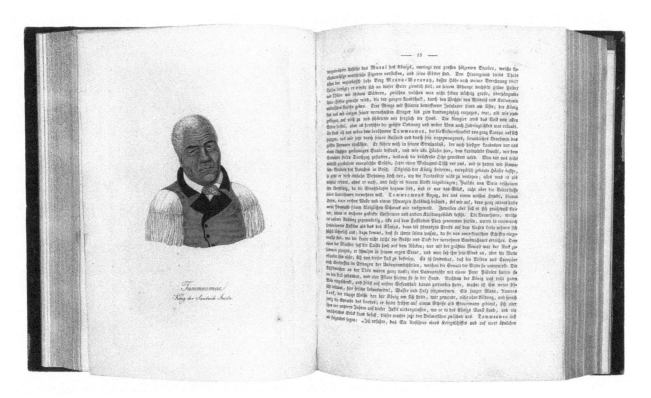

During the last years of his life, Kamehameha spent most of his time in Kailua on the Kona coast of the Big Island. He is remembered for uniting the islands and bringing them peace. In this portrait, Kamehameha chose to pose in western clothing, rather than in his traditional Hawaiian dress. This portrait is based on a version that was painted from life in Kailua by the Russian artist Louis Choris. Hawaiian Historical Society

People quit worshiping at *heiau* like this one soon after the death of Kamehameha I. Hawai'i State Archives

II, was born in 1796 or 1797.) The second son, born around 1814, was Kauikeaouli. The daughter, Nāhi'ena'ena, was born in 1815. Kauikeaouli later succeeded Liholiho as Kamehameha III.

During the last seven years of his life, Kamehameha spent most of his time in the settlement at Kailua on the Kona coast of the Big Island. He died there on May 8, 1819.

Although by uniting the Islands and bringing them peace he prepared the way for the missionaries, he knew little of Christian beliefs. Had he lived one more year, he would have met the first group of missionaries from New England. He would probably not have welcomed their efforts to destroy the old ways. To the very last he held firmly to the old *kapu* and the worship of the Hawaiian gods. As late as 1818 he ordered the deaths of three men for minor violations of the *kapu*. Yet, when he was dying, he would not allow priests to perform human sacrifices to speed his recovery.

The funeral rites followed the ancient customs. The

most important part of the ceremony was the disposal of the dead king's bones. This act was called *hūnākele*, which means "to hide in secret." The friend chosen to ensure that Kamehameha's remains would never be touched was Chief Hoapili. He hid them, with the help of Hoʻolulu. To this day no one knows where the bones were deposited. There is a story that years later Kamehameha III, on a visit to Kailua, persuaded Hoʻolulu to show him the spot. They began their journey to the hills together, but when Hoʻolulu saw that they were being followed, he turned back. Today, "only the stars of the heavens know the resting place of Kamehameha."

hūnākele: to hide in secret

Summing Up the Chapter

When Kamehameha's attempts to conquer Kauaʻi, the last of the major islands, failed, he devoted himself to organizing and ruling the rest of his kingdom. He used the *kapu* system to strengthen his authority. The first traders to come to the Islands were the British. They were soon followed by the Americans. The Islands were used as a place to refit ships and to stop over during the winter. Soon Hawaiians too entered into trade, exchanging provisions and sandalwood for iron, nails, tools, and cloth. As the demand for sandalwood grew, Hawaiians began to import useful and luxury articles from all over the world. Until the death of Kamehameha I, the sandalwood trade was a royal monopoly. The trade and the coming of foreigners greatly influenced the lives, health, and habits of the Islanders. Kauaʻi finally came under Kamehameha's rule when the king of that island surrendered it in 1810. A plot against Kamehameha by an agent of a Russian trading company was put down. When Kamehameha I died in 1819, he had united the Hawaiian Islands and brought them peace and progress.

4
New Beliefs

Kaʻahumanu became *kuhina nui* when Liholiho became king. During her lifetime, she proposed that the *kapu* be abolished and acted as a strong leader of the Hawaiian people. Painting by © Herb Kawainui Kāne

Liholiho was crowned King Kamehameha II in 1819. Guava Graphics

Liholiho, born in 1796 or 1797 to Kamehameha and Keōpūolani, was not given in *hānai* to another chief, as was the usual custom. Instead, he was brought up in his father's household, by Kamehameha's favorite wife, Ka'ahumanu. When Liholiho became king, in 1819, Ka'ahumanu announced that he would share the rule with her. In her role as *kuhina nui*, she had as much power as Liholiho.

The End of the *Kapu* System

For some years, belief in the *kapu* system had weakened. Even the high priest, Hewahewa, came to agree with Ka'ahumanu and the queen mother, Keōpūolani, that the old gods should be overthrown, the *heiau* burned, and the *kapu* abolished.

At this point events began to move rapidly. On the morning of Kamehameha's death, some chiefs advised Ka'ahumanu to do away with the *kapu*, but she decided that it was too soon to act. Two weeks later Liholiho was crowned at a great ceremony in Kailua. At the end of the ceremony, Ka'ahumanu proposed that the *kapu* be overthrown. The young king, who had been carefully trained in the old religion, refused to give his consent. Shortly after, Keōpūolani and her younger son, Kauikeaouli, decided to eat together

hānai: adoption

kuhina nui: prime minister

abolished: gotten rid of

Kalanimōkū (Billy Pitt), left, and John Young were trusted advisors of Kamehameha II. Hawai'i State Archives

Kalanimōkū was baptized aboard the *Uranie* by the ship's chaplain. Hawai'i State Archives

in violation of the *kapu*. The king did not object, but did not join them.

Now another event of religious importance occurred. In August 1819, the French ship *Uranie*, commanded by Captain Louis de Freycinet, dropped anchor at Kailua. He had been asked by John Young to help Liholiho maintain law and order. On a visit to the ship, Kalanimōkū, the king's adviser, asked to be baptized by the ship's chaplain. A few weeks later, when the *Uranie* reached O'ahu, Kalanimōkū's younger brother, Boki, the governor of that island, also asked to be baptized. Quite clearly the old ways were changing.

Now Ka'ahumanu and Keōpūolani put more pressure on Liholiho. After giving the matter much thought, he went with his court to Kailua, where a great feast had been prepared. Liholiho sat down and openly feasted with men and women.

When the people saw that no punishment followed his

act, they rejoiced that the *kapu* were ended. Quickly the news spread throughout the islands. People burned *heiau* and the images of gods, led by the high priest himself. This was in November 1819.

The *kapu* did not die easily, however. Some Hawaiians kept the images of their gods. Some chiefs were angry that the *kapu* had been ended. Among these was the young chief Kekuaokalani, the keeper of the war god Kūkāʻilimoku. In December a crowd of priests, chiefs, and commoners offered him the crown if it could be taken from Liholiho.

Kaʻahumanu, Kalanimōkū, and the royal party were at Kailua. They were worried by this revolt. They decided to try to settle it peaceably, if possible, or by force, if necessary. They were well supplied with arms, having bought a shipment of muskets and ammunition from an American trader some months before. Efforts to avoid fighting failed.

At Ahuʻena *heiau*, Liholiho openly feasted with men and women for the first time, breaking the kapu. RJBest, Inc.

In 1824, the high chiefess Kapiʻolani defied Pele, the volcano goddess, to show her acceptance of Christianity. She descended into the caldera of the volcano, where she ate *ʻohelo* berries without asking Pele's permission and read passages from the Bible. Unharmed, she returned home, hoping her actions would win converts among her people.
Painting by © Herb Kawainui Kāne

‘Ōpūkaha‘ia was the first Hawaiian to
travel to the United States to learn
English and study Christianity.
Kawaiaha‘o Church

Brave Hawaiians, including Kekuaokalani and his wife, died in battle. All of those who survived were finally pardoned by Liholiho.

Soon after this battle the king sent one of his chiefs to put down a revolt of the people of Hāmākua. The revolt was quickly ended, and the ancient gods of the Hawaiians were no more. But little did the Hawaiians know that, as they fought this last battle, the servants of a new god, the god of the Christians, were on their way to the Sandwich Islands.

The Story of ‘Ōpūkaha‘ia

In 1808 a sixteen-year-old Hawaiian boy named Henry ‘Ōpūkaha‘ia swam out to an American ship anchored in Kealakekua Bay and begged the master, Captain Brintnall, to take him to America. Orphaned in one of the tribal wars, he had resolved to seek a new home in a foreign land.

Although Brintnall already had one Hawaiian cabin boy, he agreed to take ‘Ōpūkaha‘ia with him on his return trip. Pleased by ‘Ōpūkaha‘ia's progress in learning English, Brintnall took the boy into his home in New Haven, Connecticut.

‘Ōpūkaha‘ia (also known as Obookiah) was found one evening on the campus of Yale college in tears. On being asked why he was crying, he replied that "nobody gave him learning." Several of the students undertook to teach him, and a Yale professor took him into his home. There he learned and accepted the basic beliefs of Christianity. He wanted to take the message of his new faith to his native Hawai‘i. This inspired the American Board of Commissioners for Foreign Missions, in Boston, to start a missionary school in Connecticut for the "education of heathen youth." ‘Ōpūkaha‘ia and several other youths then in New England entered this school.

‘Ōpūkaha‘ia never achieved his dream of returning to Hawai‘i. In February 1818 he died of typhus fever and was buried in Connecticut.

The Arrival of the Missionaries

In October 1819 the board organized the first group of missionaries to the Hawaiian Islands. On October 23 they sailed from Boston in the *Thaddeus* on a painful and

PIONEER COMPANY

Brig Thaddeus, 164 days from Boston. Arrived at Kailua, April 4, 1820. Landed at Honolulu, April 19, 1820.

Rev. Hiram Bingham Mrs. Sybil (Moseley) Bingham

Mr. Samuel Ruggles

Mrs. Nancy (Wells) Ruggles

Rev. Asa Thurston Mrs. Lucy (Goodale) Thurston

Capt. Daniel Chamberlain

Mrs. Mercy (Partridge) Whitney
Mrs. Jerusha (Burnett) Chamberlain

Mr. Samuel Whitney
Mr. Elisha Loomis

Dr. Thomas Holman Mrs. Lucia (Ruggles) Holman
Mrs. Maria Theresa (Sartwell) Loomis

Mrs. Holman Tomlinson

Pioneer missionaries. Hawai'i State Archives

exhausting 160-day voyage around Cape Horn. By midcentury, eleven other groups followed.

exhausting: very tiring

The seventeen members of the first group were led by two ministers, the Reverend Hiram Bingham and the Reverend Asa Thurston. Samuel Whitney and Samuel Ruggles were teachers. Dr. Thomas Holman was a physician. Daniel Chamberlain was a farmer. Elisha Loomis was a printer. Their wives were expected to serve as teachers. Three young Hawaiians came with them: William Kanui, John Honoli'i, and Thomas Hopu. Also among the passengers were the five Chamberlain children and George Kaumuali'i, a son of the high chief of Kaua'i. At the age of six, Kaumuali'i had been sent to Boston to be educated.

The missionaries, who differed in talents and temperaments, had been given a difficult assignment. They were to farm and build houses, schools, and churches. They were to learn the language of the people and teach them to read the

temperaments: personalities, characters

41

Bible. Above all, they were to lead the Hawaiians away from their old religion.

On March 30, 1820, the *Thaddeus* anchored at Kawaihae on the Big Island. Messengers went ashore to find out what had been happening. They returned with the news that Kamehameha was dead and that Liholiho had abolished the *kapu*. The missionaries saw this as proof that God had blessed their plans.

Learning that the king and chiefs were at Kailua, the captain sailed there. Bingham and Thurston were greeted by Kalanimōkū. After they called on Kuakini, the governor, and John Young, the king's adviser, they were allowed to meet with Liholiho. They gave him gifts, and asked for permission to stay in the Islands.

For several days the king withheld his decision while he talked with the chiefs. On April 6 Bingham invited him and his queens to dine on the *Thaddeus*. The next day some of the women in the missionary party went ashore with the men. The Hawaiians had often seen *haole* men and their children by Hawaiian women, but the sight of *haole* women was new to them. Samuel Kamakau describes the excitement as the party walked along the beach:

> The people came in crowds, men, women, and children, and exclaimed over the pretty faces of the white women, their deepset eyes, their bonnets that jutted forward, their long necks which won for them the name "Long neck" ('A'ioeoe). Crowds gathered, and one and another exclaimed, "How white the women are!" . . . "What long necks! But pleasing to look at!" "What pinched-in bodies! What tight clothing above and wide below."

On the next day Bingham again pressed the king for a decision. John Young and the queen supported the missionaries' request to stay. Opposing them were some of the chiefs and a Frenchman named Jean B. Rives, who had gained a strong influence over Liholiho. Rives may have feared that the missionaries would compete with him for the

Samuel Kamakau was a well-respected Hawaiian historian who wrote about Hawaiian history and culture in the eighteenth and nineteenth centuries.
Hawai'i State Archives

influence: power, control

king's favor. He argued that the missionaries were dangerous. He said that they would try to seize the government, and that their religion was not true Christianity. Later, in Honolulu, other foreigners, traders, and whalers told the chiefs that when the missionaries dug cellars under their houses they intended to store gunpowder there to prepare for an armed uprising.

Finally the king made his decision. The doctor and one of the ministers were to stay in Kailua-Kona, but the rest could go to Honolulu. They could stay for only one year.

Encouraged by this decision, the missionaries made their plans. On April 12 the trunks, boxes, and other baggage of the Holmans, the Thurstons, William Kanui, and Thomas Hopu, who were to stay in Kailua, were brought ashore. An entry in Lucy Thurston's journal describes their first evening in their new home:

Lucy Thurston was a member of the first group of missionaries to arrive in Honolulu. Hawai'i State Archives

> At evening twilight we sundered ourselves from close family ties, from the dear old brig, and from civilization. We went ashore and entered, as our home, an abode of the most uncouth and humble character. It was a thatched hut, with one room, having two windows made simply by cutting away the thatch leaving the bare poles. On the ground for the feet was first a layer of grass, then of mats. Here we found our effects from the *Thaddeus*; but no arrangement of them could be made till the house was thoroughly cleaned.

sundered: separated

brig: a two-masted, square-sailed ship

abode: a place to live in

uncouth: rough, uncivilized

About a week later the rest of the party landed at Honolulu. Here they were welcomed by Governor Boki and by a number of *haole* residents, who gave them temporary shelter until houses could be built for them. Toward the end of April, the *Thaddeus* sailed for Kaua'i, bearing Whitney and Ruggles. They, with their wives, were to establish the first mission station on that island. Also onboard was George Kaumuali'i, eagerly looking forward to a reunion with his royal father.

In August Kalanimōkū asked that a teacher be sent to

the island of Hawai'i. Elisha Loomis, whose wife the month before had given birth to the first *haole* child born in the islands, was chosen to go. On his way he stopped at Maui to visit with the Holmans, who had moved to Lahaina without waiting for permission from the Mission. Soon after that, the Holmans were recalled to O'ahu. Since the Holmans' relations with Hiram Bingham had become strained, they moved on to Kaua'i. Now only Bingham and Chamberlain were left in Honolulu.

When their first year ended, they persuaded the king, who had moved to Honolulu by this time, to let them stay. The work of building houses, conducting religious services, and establishing schools went on at a rapid pace. In August 1821, they dedicated the first Christian church, located where Kawaiaha'o Church now stands.

Summing Up the Chapter

Largely through the influence of the two wives of Kamehameha I, the new King Liholiho soon abolished the *kapu* system. The system did not die peacefully. A Hawaiian boy, 'Ōpūkaha'ia, inspired the American Board of Commissioners for Foreign Missions to send missionaries to the Sandwich Islands. The first missionaries arrived in 1820 and after a time were given permission to stay in the Islands.

5
The Reign of Liholiho, King Kamehameha II (1819–1824)

During Liholiho's short reign as Kamehameha II, the people of Hawai'i experienced many changes. The *kapu* were abolished and the missionaries arrived, preaching a new religion. Kawaiaha'o Church

L iholiho's short reign as Kamehameha II was a time of change and uncertainty. The *kapu* system was weakening, and *haole* missionaries were preaching a new religion. Foreign ships brought new goods and deadly diseases.

Decline in the Population and Health

In the United States, the Panic of 1819 had cut off the money supply needed for trading in China, so merchants began to flood the open Hawaiian market with goods that might tempt the chiefs. In order to pay for these luxuries, the chiefs forced the people into the hills to cut and transport sandalwood. Farms were left unattended, which reduced the food supply. The people's health suffered from the long hours of labor and shortage of food.

Another blow to islanders' health was the introduction of foreigners' diseases. The high death rate in the reigns of Kamehameha II and III is described by Samuel Kamakau:

> The foreign ships which arrived at Oʻahu during Kamehameha's occupation of that island brought in many diseases, especially the severe pestilence of 1804 when so many chiefs and commoners perished. . . . In 1831 the school teachers began to take the census. Although it was not complete, they reported a little under 200,000. It is therefore evident that the population declined after the arrival of the missionaries even though all wars ceased, and robbery and murder were wiped out. . . . In 1826 thousands died, especially in the country districts, of an epidemic of "coughs, congested lungs, and sore throat." . . . In February, 1839, a ship . . . brought a pestilence from which many died, Kinau among others. In September, 1848, an American warship brought the disease known as measles to Hilo, Hawaiʻi. It spread and carried away about a third of the population. . . . Again in March and April of 1853 smallpox was discovered . . . and it broke out in Honolulu the following May. . . . Leprosy is another disease brought to this country . . . .

Panic of 1819: an economic depression sometimes called "America's first great economic crisis"

pestilence: a usually fatal disease that affects many people at the same time

census: an official count of the population

leprosy: a somewhat contagious disease that causes loss of feeling

From all these diseases the native population of these islands has suffered decrease.

Kamakau, who died in 1876, learned firsthand about the harmful effects of the foreigners' civilization. He also points to certain harmful Hawaiian behaviors that existed both before and after the arrival of the foreigners. One was infanticide. Another was the slaughter of women and children during the wars and feuds of the chiefs. Another was heavy drinking, which the Hawaiians learned from traders and whalers. By 1822 at least two distilleries had been set up, and the Hawaiians learned to make liquor from fermented sugarcane juice, sweet potatoes, or *ti* root.

infanticide: the killing of unwanted babies

feuds: disagreements that last for a long period

distilleries: places for making alcoholic beverages

fermented: changed by yeast from sugar and carbon dioxide to alcohol

The Death of Kaumuali'i

When Kaumuali'i surrendered Kaua'i in 1810, Kamehameha allowed him to remain as governor. In July 1821, Liholiho decided to test the loyalty of Kaumuali'i. He set sail for Kaua'i, accompanied by Boki, governor of O'ahu, and a few members of the royal court. On Kaua'i he was welcomed with the firing of guns and ringing of bells. Kaumuali'i treated him as an honored guest.

Kaumuali'i gave control of his lands, his armed forces, and his vessels to Liholiho. A few weeks later, as Liholiho was about to leave for O'ahu, he persuaded Kaumuali'i to board his ship and took him to Honolulu.

There, Ka'ahumanu took Kaumuali'i as her husband. He lived with her until his death in 1824. His lands on Kaua'i were redivided, and a high-ranking chief was sent to govern the island. This ended the independent kingdom of Kaua'i.

Liholiho's Journey to London

In May 1823, Keōpūolani, the king's mother and the highest-ranking chiefess in the Islands, went with missionaries William Richards and Charles Stewart to set up a mission on Maui. In August a new church was ready for dedication. Liholiho, Hiram Bingham, and all the great chiefs were present for the ceremony. Soon afterwards Keōpūolani fell ill. In September, after being baptized in the Christian faith, she died.

Before Liholiho left on his trip to England, he named his younger brother, Kauikeaouli, as his successor. Kauikeaouli was only nine years old at the time. Hawai'i State Archives

regent: someone who rules for someone else who is absent or too young

After his mother's burial, Liholiho made plans for a trip to England. He and his party sailed from Honolulu on a British whaler in late November 1823.

Before he left, Liholiho named his younger brother, Kauikeaouli, as his successor. Since the prince was only nine years old, Ka'ahumanu was named as regent, in supreme authority, and Kalanimōkū continued as prime minister.

Why did Liholiho take this voyage? He may have wanted to learn more about the foreigners' world. He also may have wanted to show the same friendship for England his father had once shown and to ask the help of England's king in the event of an enemy attack.

Among those with Liholiho on the voyage were his favorite wife, Kamāmalu; Governor Boki of O'ahu and his wife, Liliha; James Young Kaneloa, a son of John Young, who served as interpreter; and the ever present Rives.

The ship arrived in England in May, and the royal couple and their party were given rooms at a fashionable hotel. Later they were entertained by the British foreign secretary

Kamehameha II and his wife, Kamāmalu, attending a theater performance in London. Hawai'i State Archives

and other London notables. The Hawaiians were delighted with the great city and were given much attention wherever they went.

On May 31 they had seats in the royal box at Covent Garden Theater. The queen was greatly affected by the play and wept at some of the scenes. Several days later they attended another play, and at another time watched a balloon ascent.

The Deaths of Liholiho and Kamāmalu

Late in June the king and queen were to be introduced to King George. Before this could happen, however, the couple were stricken with measles. The others in the party fell ill too, but recovered. Kamāmalu died on July 8. An attending physician spoke of the king's firmness of mind in the face of his great sorrow. But the effects of his illness and the shock of his loss were too much for Liholiho to bear. Within a week he too was dead.

Many years later a Honolulu merchant, Theophilus H. Davies, at the request of then Princess Liliu'okalani, found out more about what happened following the deaths of the king and queen. His letter to the princess, dated July 26, 1889, tells the story:

> "On Saturday, July 7th, the remains lay in State in a large apartment on the ground floor of the hotel, the central part of the room was divided from the rest by a frame-work 14 feet square, open on three sides, the floor being covered with small feather cloaks, and a number of capes and helmets. The large royal cloak was at the head of the coffin.
>
> "On Sunday, July 18th, at 5 'o'clock, a hearse and six horses conveyed the coffin to St. Martin's Church, and it was deposited beside the coffin of the Queen.
>
> "On Sept. 1st, at one in the morning, it was reported that three men attempted to break into the church to steal the King's body, for which it was said 200 pounds had been offered, but every avenue to the church was strictly guarded and the men made off. On Tuesday night, 7th, at 10 o'clock, two hearses, followed by mourning coaches . . . , conveyed the remains from St. Martin's Church to the London Dock, where they were embarked onboard the Frigate 'Blonde' for conveyance to Honolulu.
>
> " . . . On Wednesday, Sept. 30th, the 'Blonde' sailed for Honolulu."

News of the king's death had been brought to Honolulu two months before the *Blonde* arrived, and memorial services were held in the Christian churches. The ship arrived in Honolulu on May 11, 1825. Funeral services were held, attended by a company of marines from the *Blonde* and by the British consul.

Former Caledonian Hotel in London, where Kamehameha II died in 1824.
Hawai'i State Archives

frigate: a high-speed, medium-sized sailing warship

consul: a person who lives in a foreign country and looks after the interests of his or her country there

On May 11, 1825, the British ship HMS *Blonde* returned Kamehameha's remains to Hawai'i, almost a year after his death. Painting by © Herb Kawainui Kāne

After the king's death and burial, the missionaries and the Congregational Church grew more important. Even though the church was opposed by foreign traders, by the end of the year most of the important Hawaiian chiefs, including Ka'ahumanu, Kalanimōkū ("Billy Pitt"), and several of the wives of the first two Kamehamehas were members.

Congregational Church: a Protestant group in which each separate church governs itself

Summing Up the Chapter

Hawai'i's population and health declined under the burden of the unlimited sandalwood trade, the introduction of the foreigners' diseases, and the habit of heavy drinking. The last king of Kaua'i, Kaumuali'i, was taken to O'ahu, where he ended his days as the husband of Ka'ahumanu. In 1823–24 Liholiho and his favorite wife, together with a few of his loyal supporters, paid a visit to London. What began as a triumph ended in tragedy when the royal couple contracted measles and died within a few days of each other.

6
Whalers and Traders (1825–1860), King Kamehameha III (1825–1854)

In the spring of 1825, ten-year-old Kauikeaouli became the new ruler of Hawai'i. During his twenty-nine-year reign, he grew into a well-respected leader who oversaw dramatic cultural, commercial, and social changes in the Islands.

Painting by©Herb Kawainui Kāne

In the spring of 1825 the young Kauikeaouli became the new king of Hawai'i. The real ruler, however, was the regent Ka'ahumanu, assisted by Kalanimōkū. She tried to deal with the disorder that arose as more and more *haole* found their way to the Islands. One of her first tasks was to enforce order in the two chief whaling ports of Honolulu and Lahaina.

Whaling now replaced the sandalwood trade as the chief source of income. After 1819 most of the whaling ships were American. They usually arrived in the Islands in March or April and left for the whaling grounds off the coast of Japan in May. In September they returned to Hawai'i to refit their ships.

The number of whalers anchored in Hawaiian ports increased rapidly. In 1830 there were 157 arrivals. By 1844 the number had tripled.

The Effects of Whaling on the Hawaiian Economy

The whaling trade was a dangerous and uncertain one. It depended upon luck and upon the changing prices for whale oil. But it had a great effect on the life of the Islands.

As one whaler after another anchored at Honolulu and Lahaina during the spring and fall, activity in the ports increased. The ships needed new provisions. Blacksmiths and carpenters stayed busy repairing hulls and deck gear damaged from long months at sea. And like sailors everywhere, the crews swarmed ashore to have fun.

The visiting seamen had a bad influence on the island social order. They brought disease, and they often behaved badly. Sailors who knowingly spread contagious diseases were punished. They were fined for carrying dangerous weapons, breaking the Sabbath, drunkenness, fighting, and other law breaking. Desertions were common, either because of the hard life aboard ship or because of the charms of Hawaiian weather and people.

Many a wild tale can be told about the sailors in the seaports of O'ahu and Maui. One of the best-known stories tells of the sailors' riot in Honolulu in 1852. A rowdy sailor named Burns was seized by constables and locked up with some of his mates. He created such a disturbance that the

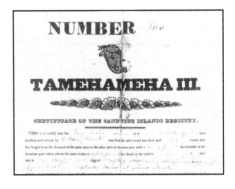

Ship registry signed by Kamehameha III (signature enlarged beneath)
Hawai'i State Archives

Sabbath: day of rest and worship

desertion: leaving one's job on a ship

53

The whaling industry replaced the sandalwood trade in Hawai'i and brought seamen from all over the world to Hawai'i's shores. As a result, the population grew and an increased need for goods and services developed. The production of cattle, salt, and agriculture increased. Painting by © Herb Kawainui Kāne

When sailors broke the law, they served time in Hale Pa'ahao prison in Lahaina, Maui. RJBest, Inc.

constable hit him on the head with a club to quiet him. Unfortunately, he hit him too hard, and he died a few hours later.

The next day a group of sailors demanded that the constable be punished. Their demand was refused. After Burns's funeral the next day, they poured into the streets, armed with knives and clubs, and finally set fire to the police station. The flames spread to two nearby buildings and destroyed them. The fire also threatened the oil-laden whale ships anchored closely together in the harbor. All that day and evening the mob terrorized the town.

The next day, because of the danger to the fleet, the ships' officers joined with the police and civilians to end the riot. Under the governor's orders, the islanders and the armed police cleared the streets.

The whaling trade brought more than just trouble to the Islands. For one thing, the production of cattle and salt increased. The cattle that Vancouver had brought to the

Islands had multiplied into large herds in the mountains and inland plains. The king and the chiefs sold or leased to ambitious *haole* the right to shoot the cattle. The meat was salted and sold in large quantities to the ship owners. In the 1830s a man from Massachusetts, John Parker, started one of the world's great cattle-raising centers, the Parker Ranch on the Big Island. At first the salt was gathered in small amounts in tidepools, but later it was dug from the bottom of Salt Lake near Honolulu and ground in a wind-powered mill.

Agricultural production was also encouraged. The Irish potato was introduced by 1830 and grown in the Kula district of Maui. Also in demand were coffee, pumpkins, cabbages, breadfruit, taro, bananas, arrowroot, melons, pineapples, and firewood.

Another side effect was the increasing use of young Hawaiians as crewmen on the whalers. In this way they became better acquainted with the ways of foreigners and with foreign ports. The enlistment of Hawaiians was caused partly by the frequent desertions of seamen, especially in slack seasons. So many Hawaiians were being enlisted that

John Parker, a Massachusetts native, started one of the world's greatest cattle-raising centers, the Parker Ranch on the Big Island. Hawai'i State Archives

ambitious: wanting to have more money or power

tidepools: water that collects in rocky hollows at the shoreline at low tide

arrowroot: a plant whose root is used to make a starch for food

In 1847, John Parker and his two sons built Mana Hale, the original Parker Ranch homestead. Hawai'i State Archives

Sugarcane. B. Bess

Coffee. Ross Wilson, Current Events

Sugar and coffee have been important agricultural products in Hawai'i since the 1860s.

a law passed in 1859 provided that no islander could be shipped without permission of the governor of an island under penalty of a $500 fine.

The whaling trade increased the importance of seaport cities. As whales became scarcer and more difficult to catch, ships were forced to make longer voyages and to depend upon Hawai'i for refitting and provisioning. All of this brought profit to island merchants.

The Decline of Whaling

The boom period of Hawaiian whaling lasted from 1840 to 1860. By 1840 new fishing grounds in the Kodiak area (near Alaska) were being exploited. In 1848 the grounds in the Arctic Ocean north of the Bering Strait were discovered. Although there was a slow period at the time of the California gold rush, prices of whale oil and bone remained high until the Civil War.

The Civil War changed whaling. The whaling fleet was seriously damaged by privateers, which reportedly sank about fifty ships. As the war went on, competition from petroleum caused whale oil prices to drop. Perhaps the most important reason for the decay of the industry was that the cost of voyages was increasing as the herds of whales were decreasing.

The whaling industry suffered a final destructive blow in 1871. Thirty-three out of forty whale ships that had entered the Arctic Ocean in the spring of that year were caught in the ice and destroyed. Only one of the seven Hawaiian whalers escaped. In addition to the loss of the cargoes, there was a huge loss to Honolulu merchants who had expected to provision the ships.

During the 1860s, as the number of whaling vessels decreased, business slackened in the Hawaiian Islands. Efforts to find new sources of income led to experiments in increasing the production of silk, cotton, rice, sugar, and coffee. Only the last two continued to be important in the local economy.

The Growth of Trading

Throughout the long reign of Kamehameha III, Hawai'i grew more important as a center for transpacific business.

STREET VIEW AT HONOLULU.

Between 1830 and 1840, the population of Honolulu grew. By 1840, Honolulu had a population of about seven thousand, and the settlements of Lahaina on Maui, Hilo on Hawaiʻi, and Waimea on Kauaʻi were large enough to be called towns. Hawaiʻi State Archives

In the early part of this period, trading vessels sailed between the Latin American countries on the Pacific coast and trading ports in Asia and the East Indies, stopping in Hawaiʻi to refuel and take on supplies. As time went on, a lively trade also developed with the Russians in Alaska and Kamchatka and with the Spanish settlements in California.

This general Pacific trade, in addition to the business in fur, sandalwood, and whale products, led to the growth of a stable business community in Hawaiʻi. By 1830 Honolulu was no longer a straggling village. It was large enough to support a dozen merchants with their clerks; twenty liquor dealers and innkeepers; and fifty cooks, carpenters, blacksmiths, tailors, sailmakers, caulkers, herdsmen, and farmers. Ten years later, in 1840, Honolulu had a population of about seven thousand. The settlements of Lahaina on Maui, Hilo on Hawaiʻi, and Waimea on Kauaʻi were large enough to be called towns. At least four Hawaiian merchants had branches in the smaller community of San Francisco on the mainland.

The increase in trade between the Islands and England and the United States led these countries to appoint consuls

ap: a term that in Welsh names means "son of"

to represent their countrymen in Honolulu. Some of the early consuls did not represent their countries wisely.

Unsolved problems, such as the payment of debts and the conduct of seamen, caused President John Quincy Adams to send a man-of-war to Honolulu in 1826. The commander, Thomas ap Catesby Jones, was told to promote friendly relations with the island's rulers and to arrange for the protection of American nationals and trade. In his stay of less than three months, he helped settle the long-standing feud between the missionaries and the majority of the other foreigners in Honolulu. He arranged for a debt settlement approved by the chiefs and their *haole* creditors. Finally, he proposed the "articles of arrangement," for the protection of American trade. These articles were signed in December 1826. They required the Hawaiian government to prevent desertions from American ships, to not favor one nation over another in regard to tariffs and other charges, and to help recover goods from wrecked vessels.

tariffs: taxes on imported goods

Although the United States Senate never officially accepted this treaty, it served as a working agreement for more than ten years. The efforts of Captain Jones helped increase American influence in a kingdom where the British had been the most influential foreigners since the time of Kamehameha I.

Governor Boki

Not all of the shipping and trading was done by foreigners. The king and chiefs owned and operated a number of small brigs and schooners manned partly by Hawaiians. These ships traveled between the islands, and several made trips to the Russian settlements in North America, to Manila, and to Hong Kong. The most active native trader was Governor Boki of Oʻahu. He engaged in trade partly for his own gain and partly to get funds to pay off debts of government chiefs during the reign of Liholiho. By the time Kamehameha III came to the throne, these debts, owed mostly to American traders, were a heavy burden for the kingdom.

In 1827 Boki bought the cargo of an English trading ship and opened a retail store in Honolulu. He converted part of the building into a hotel. He named it "The Blonde"

Governor Boki and his wife, Liliha. Hawai'i State Archives

after the English frigate that had brought him home from England several years earlier. He also entered into several overseas trading ventures, none of them very successful.

Late in 1829 a report reached Honolulu that excited Boki. He learned that sandalwood could be gathered easily on the island of Eromanga in the New Hebrides. Heavily in debt and in disfavor with Ka'ahumanu, Boki decided to leave Hawai'i and seek his fortune elsewhere. He fitted out two of the king's brigs, the *Kamehameha* and the *Becket*. Loading them with four to five hundred of his followers and friends, he sailed to the southern islands.

From the beginning the trip was mismanaged. The two brigs met at an island near Fiji. Boki, aboard the *Kamehameha*, decided to go on ahead of the *Becket*. At the last moment he took onboard a large number of islanders to help cut the sandalwood he hoped to find. The ship was

New Hebrides: islands northeast of Australia known today as Vanuatu

59

never seen or heard of again. Was there a mutiny? an explosion? a violent storm? Nobody knows, and the fate of Boki remains a mystery.

The *Becket* reached Eromanga and stayed there about five weeks. No sandalwood was cut since the islanders were unfriendly and many of the crew died of disease. The survivors began the long journey back to Hawai'i. Starvation, disease, and violence cut down the seamen one by one. When the ship reached Honolulu in August 1830, only twenty men were onboard, including eight foreigners who had joined the ill-fated expedition.

Effects of the Death of Ka'ahumanu

In June 1832 Ka'ahumanu became ill and died at her home in Mānoa Valley in Honolulu. Chiefs and commoners, as well as the missionaries she had supported, mourned her death. Kīna'u, a wife and half-sister of Liholiho, became *kuhina nui,* with the title of Ka'ahumanu II. She also served as governor of O'ahu and as regent until the king became of age.

In March 1833, Kauikeaouli announced that he was of age and would take charge of the kingdom. He brought back many of the old customs, including the hula. In 1835, under pressure from Kīna'u, the missionaries, and some of the chiefs, he agreed to share power with Kīna'u and the Council of Chiefs. Because the king was young and Kīna'u lacked the strength and political skill of Ka'ahumanu I, for several years the kingdom suffered from lack of strong leadership.

As he grew older, Kamehameha III became a stronger ruler and earned the respect and love of his people. During the last twenty years of his reign, a strong Polynesian monarchy changed into a modern constitutional monarchy in which *haole* advisers and lawmakers played a leading part. Other developments in the reign of Kamehameha III—land reform, the spread of education, the ambitions of foreign nations, the growth of a great plantation system—are described in later chapters.

In the years following the death of Ka'ahumanu, the traders and promoters, chiefly American and British, began to build a stable business community. C. Brewer & Company started in connection with trade in sandalwood in 1826.

constitutional: based on a constitution, or written laws

Kamehameha III brought back many customs to the people of Hawaiʻi, including the hula. These dancers were photographed in the 1860s. Hawaiʻi State Archives

A branch of Hudson's Bay Company came to Honolulu in 1834. In 1849 a German, Captain H. Hackfeld, started a firm that developed into American Factors, Ltd.

In addition to the descendants of the missionaries, such as the Baldwins, Rices, Cookes, and Wilcoxes, many other young *haole* men began to establish firms that are well known today.

Charles Reed Bishop, a New Yorker, arrived in Hawaiʻi in 1846. He went to work for the American firm Ladd & Company and later for the kingdom as a customs collector. In 1850 he married one of the descendants of Kamehameha I, Bernice Pauahi. She was one of the largest landholders in the kingdom. In 1858 he and a partner started Bishop & Company (now known as First Hawaiian Bank), the first permanent bank to do business in Hawaiʻi. At first he financed the whale oil business. After the reciprocity treaty

Charles Reed Bishop. Guava Graphics

prosper: become richer or more
successful

arable: fit for crops to grow in

capital: money that can be used to
make more money

Bishop & Company was the first permanent bank to do business in Hawai'i.
It was started by Charles Reed Bishop
and a partner in 1858. Today, it is
known as First Hawaiian Bank. Hawai'i
State Archives

(see chapter 13), Bishop's banking business grew rapidly
while he helped finance the sugar industry.

During the reigns of the first three Kamehamehas, it
was never clear what industry or product would best help
the country grow and prosper. One crop, however, began to
stand out. It needed plenty of arable, irrigated land, technical know-how, a stable market, a supply of labor and capital,
and a favorable political situation. This crop was sugar (see
chapter 9). Alexander and Baldwin, Ltd., began about 1870
as an informal partnership between Samuel T. Alexander
and Henry P. Baldwin. This business began not as a store
but as a plantation development on Maui. The work of the
two young partners and their success in constructing the
famous Hāmākua Ditch for the irrigation of their sugar
lands is told in chapter 13.

Summing Up the Chapter

Kīna'u succeeded Ka'ahumanu as regent until
Kauikeaouli became of age and ruled as Kamehameha III.
When he began his reign, whaling had replaced the sandalwood trade as the chief source of income. It provided
business for Hawaiian merchants, but the visiting seamen
brought sickness to Hawai'i's people. Whaling began to
decline in the 1860s. The king and some of the chiefs, as
well as foreigners, engaged in trade and shipping. Governor
Boki of O'ahu died on an expedition to the South Pacific in
search of a new source of sandalwood. Some of the problems
between the United States and Hawai'i resulting from trade
were solved during the visit of the American Captain Jones.
Many present-day Hawaiian businesses began during the
period of the early and middle 1800s.

A Bit of Harbor History

Honolulu Harbor was known to foreign mariners in the late 1700s, but was thought to be navigable only by light boats and canoes. The first ship to negotiate the entrance was a British schooner, late in 1794, a few months before the battle of Nuʻuanu.

Eventually the harbor became a busy, noisy port of call and a winter haven for sailing ships in the Pacific trade.

haven: a safe place

To provide a place for ships to dock, a wharf was built in 1825. In those early days ships entered the harbor under full sail. Lines were thrown to Hawaiians who towed the ship in. The tow path was along Richards Street. It was the only straight street in the waterfront area. Oxen and later a steam tug were used for towing. In later years, an area between Fort and Alakea Streets was filled in to provide additional wharfage.

SANDWICH ISLAND

LICENCE.

Suffer the Ship or Vessel called the *Waverly*

——————— to pass without molestation or hindrance : the said vessel is

Seventy Seven feet long, *Twenty one* feet broad and measures

One hundred forty ones 45/95 ——————

Tons, has *No* ——————— head *No* ——

Quarter Galleries, has *a Square* ——— Stern and is *Brigantine*

——————— Rigged ——————— and is the property of

Tamēahmeah the third King of the Sandwich Islands

And whereof ——————— is master.

Given under my hand at

Oahu, this **3d** day of *December* 1832

Port Captain.

Left) Sandwich Island ship license issued to King Kamehameha from the port captain on December 3, 1832.
Hawaii State Archives

63

The first book was printed in Hawai'i in 1823. Tortoiseshell was used for its binding. Hawaiian Historical Society

Long before the missionaries gave them a written language and a foreign curriculum, Hawaiians had an educational system of their own. It was based not on books but on practical needs. It taught vocational skills and the arts of navigation and warfare, the legends and history of the people, and religious and social customs.

The *ali'i*, held in great honor, received careful training. The *maka'āinana* learned skills they would need in everyday life. They learned these from the *kāhuna*—the expert canoe builders, medicine men, genealogists, navigators, farmers, house builders, and priests.

Some sort of group teaching probably existed. Many people were taught and trained at home. Others learned by watching craftspeople and *kāhuna* at work.

vocational: work-related

ali'i: chiefs

maka'āinana: common people

genealogists: people who study family histories

The Tasks of the Missionaries

Because the Protestant missionaries wanted Hawaiians to read the Bible, their first task was to teach them to read. They invented a written Hawaiian language, started a school system, and provided a printing press.

The work of the missionaries in developing education in Hawai'i can be divided into three periods. From 1820 to 1831, the Hawaiian language was written down. Textbooks were printed, and adults learned simple reading and writing. From 1831 to 1840, teachers were trained, and schools for children were started. From 1840 to 1863, the missionaries gradually gave up their control of education. The government started a number of public schools.

Some of the *haole* living in the Islands were opposed to education for Hawaiians. Even before 1820 a *haole* sailor named Archibald Campbell, who attempted to teach a chief to read, was opposed by Isaac Davis. "They will soon know more than ourselves," complained Davis. Some of the traders accused the missionaries of using religion to win control of the Islands for themselves.

Despite all obstacles, the missionaries plunged ahead. The first school was at Kailua, on the island of Hawai'i. Kamehameha II, his two queens, and his brother Kauikeaouli, then about five years old, were among the students. At Kawaihae, Kalanimōkū and a few of his followers were taught by one of the missionaries. At Honolulu, Hiram Bingham and his wife held the first quarterly "examination." At Waimea, Kaua'i, King Kaumuali'i helped the missionaries start a school in which he was the first student enrolled. Within four months of their arrival, the missionaries had started four schools.

The missionaries soon saw that they could not wait for the Hawaiians to learn English. The Bible would have to be taught in the Hawaiian language. The work of translation began, but it was not until the arrival of the Reverend William Ellis in 1822 that real progress was made. Ellis stopped in the Islands on his way to the Marquesas. Having had years of preaching experience in the Society Islands, he knew the language of Tahiti, which is closely related to Hawaiian. He was soon able to speak in Hawaiian, and this skill was of great help to the missionaries in writing down the language.

pī'āpā: alphabet

An alphabet (*pī'āpā*) of twelve letters was selected, and

The Mission Press printed the first books used in Hawai'i. Mission Houses Museum

The first missionary schools were attended by people of all ages. Hawai'i State Archives

the work of translation went on. On January 7, 1822, the first publication in Hawaiian came off the small press owned by the missionaries. Chief Ke'eaumoku made the first copy. The material was a small printed page. Later it went into an eight-page pamphlet containing the alphabet, a spelling exercise, and a few simple sentences and verses.

The history of the Mission Press is an interesting one. As the mission expanded during the 1820s and 1830s, the press produced primers, hymn books, government proclamations, and job printing for traders. In 1838 it produced the *Hawaiian Spectator*, the first quarterly review in the Pacific Ocean area. Within a few years the chiefs became enthusiastic about teaching the *palapala* to the common people.

Early Missionary Schools

The early missionary schools were very simple, both in equipment and in subjects taught. Classes were called together not by ringing a bell but by blowing on a conch shell. Pupils sat on blocks of dried bricks covered with mats. Laura Fish Judd described the annual exhibition of all the schools on O'ahu, held in April 1828.

primers: elementary textbooks for teaching children to read

proclamations: official public announcements

job printing: small printing projects such as flyers and cards

seminary: a school, usually for training ministers

palapala: printed matter

exhibition: show

procession: a group moving in an orderly, formal manner

konohiki: headman of an *ahupua'a*, or land section

kīhei: cape made of *kapa* (bark cloth), worn over one shoulder and tied in a knot

pā'ū: *kapa* (bark cloth) skirt

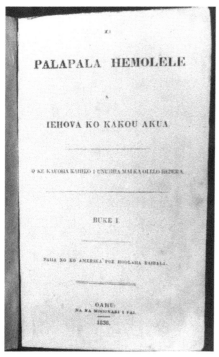

A page from the first Bible printed in Hawai'i, in 1839. Hawaiian Historical Society

genealogies: family trees, showing the descent of families from their ancestors; family histories

Adults compose these schools, as the children are not yet tamed. The people come from each district in the procession, headed by the principal man of the land (*konohiki*), all dressed in one uniform color of native cloth. One district would be clad in red, another in bright yellow, another in pure white, another in black or brown. The dress was one simple garment, the "kīhei" for men, and the "pau" for women.

It is astonishing how so many have learned to read with so few books. They teach each other, making use of banana leaves, smooth stones, and the wet sand on the sea beach, as tablets. Some read equally well with the book upside down or sidewise, as four or five of them learn from the same book with one teacher, crowding around him as closely as possible.

The aged are fond of committing to memory, and repeating in concert. . . . Their power of memory is wonderful, acquired, as I suppose, by the habit of committing and reciting traditions, and the genealogies of their kings and priests.

As yet, only portions of the Bible are translated and printed. These are demanded in sheets still wet from the press. . . .

The children are considered bright, but too wild to be brought into the schools. We intend, however, to try them very soon.

~*Honolulu: Sketches of Life in the Hawaiian Islands,* reprinted from the *Honolulu Star-Bulletin,* 1928.

As the number of schools increased, the missionaries and their wives could not do all the teaching themselves. As soon as pupils learned to read, they were sent out to teach others. After 1824, the *ali'i* also helped. Ka'ahumanu issued a proclamation saying that all Hawaiians must learn the *palapala*. Keōpūolani, the queen mother, and her husband,

Hoapili, governor of Maui, furthered the work on that island. Another worker on Maui was David Malo, who later became the first superintendent of schools in the Islands.

The American Board sent out more missionaries to start new schools. The missionary system reached its peak in 1832, when about 40 percent of the people of Hawai'i were enrolled in nine hundred schools throughout the Islands. Attendance dropped after that year for a number of reasons. A complete reorganization of the whole educational system was needed, with special attention to teaching children, finding qualified teachers, and building permanent schools.

David Malo, an accomplished Hawaiian scholar and historian, was the first superintendent of schools in the Islands. Hawaiian Historical Society

*Ka Lama Hawai*i was the first newspaper printed in Hawai'i and the first newspaper printed west of the Rocky Mountains.
Hawaiian Historical Society

Lahainaluna Seminary

At the general meeting of the mission in June 1831, the members gave serious thought to the proper training of teachers and preachers to serve in the Islands. They chose Lahainaluna on Maui as the location of a high school or seminary. In September 1831, the school, built on a thousand-acre grant from Governor Hoapili, received its first students.

Historically, Lahainaluna is one of the most interesting schools in Hawai'i. After classes in printing had been held for about a year, the press turned out a newspaper, *Ka Lama Hawai'i*, which has been called the first newspaper west

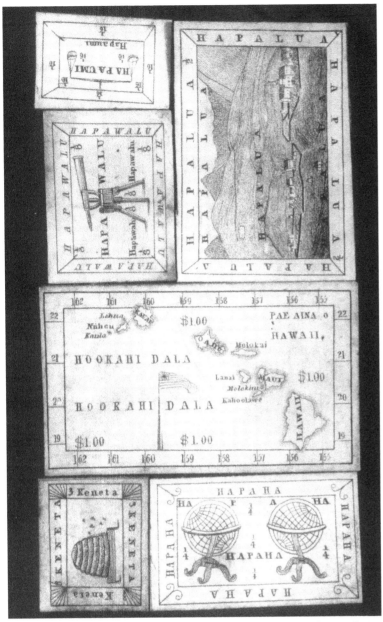

Currency used at Lahainaluna on Maui. Notice how "dollar" is spelled "dala." Hawai'i State Archives

of the Rocky Mountains. In 1843, the Reverend Sheldon Dibble, one of the original teachers of the school, produced, with his students, the first published history of the Hawaiian Islands. He also helped organize the first Hawaiian Historical Society.

Gradually control passed from the missionaries to the government. The school is now part of the public school system of Hawai'i.

Hilo Boarding School

In Hilo a similar school was opened by another early missionary, David Lyman. On a forty-acre grant of land given by the chiefs, Mr. Lyman built Hilo Boarding School. It consisted of two grass huts. There were only eight boys in the first class, which opened in 1836. The school was soon so successful that a board of trustees was chosen to guide it, and a few years later it received a charter from the government.

The wives of the Hilo missionaries helped in the work of the school. Mrs. Titus Coan opened a boarding school for girls in 1838. The Hawaiians cut timber and put up a simple building, which took care of twenty girls from seven to ten years of age. It was supported by the neighbors, who brought in weekly supplies of taro, potatoes, bananas, and fish. In his book *Life in Hawaii,* Titus Coan describes his wife's work at the school:

The Reverend David Lyman opened the Hilo Boarding School in 1836.
Hawai'i State Archives

toiled: worked hard

rudiments: basic skills

> Little gifts of money were sometimes made by strangers who came to Hilo, by officers of whale ships and men-of-war; or a piece of print or brown cotton was given, and thus the real wants of the school were supplied. Mrs. Coan toiled faithfully from day to day, in spite of pressing cares, teaching her charges the rudiments of necessary book knowledge, and of singing, sewing, washing and ironing, gardening, and other things.

Punahou School

Punahou School, on about eighty acres of land in Mānoa, O'ahu, is one of the most respected schools in the nation. It includes classes from kindergarten through twelfth grade. By 1962 it was the largest independent college preparatory school west of the Rockies.

The school was founded to provide education for the children of the missionaries. Because they were too busy with other duties to train their own children, the missionaries had only two choices: to continue sending the children across the seas to New England or to start a school in Hawai'i.

Punahou School was founded to provide education for the children of the missionaries. Hawai'i State Archives

In 1829 Ka'ahumanu spoke to Hoapili about giving Mr. Bingham some land for the use of the mission. He suggested the Punahou land, which he had given his daughter Liliha, the wife of Governor Boki of O'ahu. She did not want to give up the land, but Boki agreed to give it to Bingham.

The first plan was to build a school for Hawaiians on the land, but there was not enough money. In 1841 money was set aside to build Punahou School. The head of the school was Daniel Dole. He was the father of Sanford Dole, later to become president of the Republic of Hawai'i and first governor of the Islands as an American territory.

Chief's Children's School

In 1839 the Chief's Children's School (later called Royal School), was opened. It was a boarding school run by Mr. and Mrs. Amos S. Cooke. All the future rulers of Hawai'i attended this school.

Catholic Schools

St. Louis College, the oldest Catholic school in Hawai'i, was organized under Bishop Maigret in 1880. In 1883 it was turned over to the Brothers of Mary. Other Catholic schools are St. Joseph's in Hilo, St. Anthony's on Maui, and the schools under the Maryknoll order.

The Kamehameha Schools

The Kamehameha Schools, founded in 1887, were started with funds provided by Princess Pauahi, a descendant of Kamehameha I. She married Charles R. Bishop in 1850. Since they had no children, they decided to use the estate for the benefit of the children of Hawai'i. After Mrs. Bishop's death in 1884, the estate was run by a board of trustees of which her husband was a member.

The Kamehameha Schools, founded in 1887, were started with funds provided by Princess Pauahi Bishop, who married Charles Bishop in 1850.
Guava Graphics

On his deathbed, Kamehameha V asked High Chiefess Bernice Pauahi Bishop to be his successor. Although she was the last living descendant of Kamehameha I, she refused to accept his offer. Pauahi is remembered for her generosity and interest in helping the children of Hawai'i. Painting by © Herb Kawainui Kāne

The first Kamehameha Schools campus is now home to the Bishop Museum, founded by Charles Bishop in 1889 in honor of his late wife Princess Pauahi Bishop. Hawai'i State Archives

Three years later, in 1887, the board opened the boys' division of the school. The girls' school opened in 1894 with twenty-seven girls enrolled.

'Iolani School and St. Andrew's Priory

'Iolani School was established by the Anglicans. In 1863, Father William R. Scott began Lua'ehu School in Lahaina, Maui. The school moved to Honolulu in the early 1870s and was named 'Iolani by Queen Emma. The Anglicans also established St. Andrew's Priory for girls.

The Bishop Museum today. B. Bess

Other Private Schools

Many other schools were founded or influenced by the missionaries. Some passed from the scene. Others were combined or reorganized under new names. All of them were helpful in preparing the way for public secondary education, in furnishing vocational training, and in training the leaders of Hawai'i.

Public Education and the Constitution of 1840

Rapidly changing political conditions in the early years of the reign of Kamehameha III called for a more highly organized educational system. The missionaries could not meet the need alone.

The first important step in the development of public schools was the Constitution of 1840. This document was largely the work of William Richards, a Lahaina missionary. He was the first minister for public instruction, until his death in 1847. He was replaced by Richard Armstrong, another missionary. Armstrong was so successful in his thirteen years as minister that he has been called "the father of American education in Hawai'i." He improved teacher training, inspected schools, held examinations, and secured public lands for schools. In addition, he tried to settle religious differences between Catholic and Protestant missionaries and served as the king's agent in chartering private and select schools.

The Common Schools

Under the leadership of Richard Armstrong, Hawai'i developed a strong program of public education. The Education Act of 1850 set aside one-twentieth of all government land for the support of education. All taxable males had to pay a school tax, except schoolteachers, inspectors and school trustees, aged and infirm people, missionaries and two of their servants, constables, soldiers, and certain others. In 1855 another act placed the control of public education in the hands of a board of education with Armstrong as its president. During this period local school boards existed, but they did not remain a part of the Hawaiian school system.

At first the common schools were grass huts without floors or equipment. The teachers provided most of the materials used for teaching. Instruction was in Hawaiian as were the textbooks, which were printed at Lahainaluna. Under Armstrong's leadership better textbooks were supplied, the quality of teaching was improved, and better schoolhouses were built. The pupils were taught reading, writing, arithmetic, geography, and singing. Above all, they were taught to be God-fearing citizens. Armstrong believed

Fort Street School opened as an English day school in 1865. Hawai'i State Archives

that pupils should spend part of each school day working with their hands, particularly in school gardens.

Toward the end of Armstrong's career, a number of important changes took place in public education. The laws of 1859 required the teaching of reading, writing, arithmetic, and other similar elementary subjects. All taxable males now had to pay a school tax of two dollars. Separate schools to teach English to Hawaiians were established. Lahainaluna became part of the public school system. The Oahu Charity School, for the education of Caucasian-Hawaiian children, was turned over to the Honolulu district superintendent. It was one of the earliest schools set up in Hawai'i. Both Pohukaina School and McKinley High School stem from the Oahu Charity School. The Chief's Children's School was made a teacher training school.

By 1860 the common schools were responsible for much of public education. In 1863, three years after Armstrong's death, the American Board of Missions withdrew from education activities in Hawai'i. The descendants of the missionaries turned their attention from religion and education to business.

descendants: those who come after; children, grandchildren

77

Hawai'i's First Newspapers

The first edition of the *Honolulu Advertiser* was printed on July 2, 1856. Today, it remains the most widely read newspaper in Hawai'i.
Honolulu Advertiser

The *Evening Bulletin* and the *Hawaiian Star* merged to form today's *Honolulu Star-Bulletin*. Honolulu Star-Bulletin

The growth of newspapers is also a part of the growth of education in any community. The first English-language newspaper was the *Sandwich Island Gazette and Journal of Commerce.*

The first issue of the *Sandwich Island Gazette* came off the press on July 30, 1836. It was a four-page Saturday weekly printed on Chinese wrapping paper. The subscription cost was six dollars a year, which could be paid in cash or in goods. To fill space, the editor, twenty-two-year-old Stephen D. Mackintosh, had to depend on months-old world newspapers, local shipping notices, and contributions from his readers. Like most editors, he fought for special causes and for community improvements. His favorite cause was raising money for the Oahu Charity School, founded and supported by traders for all children not in the American Mission schools.

Another noteworthy paper was the *Polynesian*, a four-column, four-page weekly that first appeared in June 1840. Its editor was a young Bostonian named James Jackson Jarves. It was a better paper than the *Gazette*, but it was dropped after eighteen months for lack of support. In 1844 it reappeared as a government newspaper, perhaps to balance the opinions in S. C. Damon's *The Friend*, which was sometimes critical of royal policies. Jarves once more was the editor until he left the Islands in 1848. Jarves is remembered also as the author of *History of the Hawaiian or Sandwich Islands*. A series of editors managed the *Polynesian* until it was finally discontinued in 1864.

During the 1840s a number of papers appeared briefly. Among them were the *Cascade*, the *Monitor,* the *Fountain*, and the *Honolulu Times*.

The oldest paper in Hawai'i with an unbroken record down to the present is the *Advertiser*. The first copy came off the press on July 2, 1856, under the editorship of Henry M. Whitney. He named his paper the *Pacific Commercial Advertiser*, a weekly with three pages in English and one in Hawaiian. (Mr. Whitney also started a Hawaiian paper, *Ka Nupepa Kuokoa,* or *The Independent*.) The *Advertiser* had various owners, including Claus Spreckels, the "sugar king" (see chapter 13). His editor was Walter Murray Gibson, who later became prime minister under King Kalākaua. In 1882 the *Advertiser* became a daily.

The first daily paper in Hawai'i was the *Daily Hawaiian Herald,* started in 1866. The first daily to live on to the present was the *Evening Bulletin*. It later joined with the *Hawaiian Star* to form today's *Star-Bulletin*. The *Bulletin* appeared on April 24, 1882. One week later the *Advertiser* came out as a daily.

Summing Up the Chapter

Before the coming of the *haole,* the Hawaiians had a simple educational system suited to their needs. The early missionaries wrote down the Hawaiian language and taught Hawaiians to read. The printing press helped them spread learning more quickly. The first school was in Kailua, Hawai'i. Other missionary schools were established throughout the Islands. Some of those schools still exist. When the need arose for a more highly organized school system, the government stepped in. Hawai'i had one of the first state departments of instruction. In 1840, the new constitution aided the development of public schools. One of the first ministers for public instruction in the king's cabinet was Richard Armstrong, Hawai'i's "father of education." The first English-language newspaper appeared in 1836.

Hawaiian historian David Malo drew this map in 1832. Maps created during this period helped Hawaiians learn more about the world at large. Hawaiian Historical Society

8
Foreign Entanglements

During the reign of Kamehameha III, as trade grew and as more and more foreigners arrived in Hawai'i, problems involving other nations arose.

As we have seen, Hawai'i's first knowledge of the Western world came with the visits of English explorers. Later, other Englishmen—Vancouver, Davis, Young, and others—became friends and advisers to Kamehameha I. Both Kamehameha I and II looked upon the English king as the protector of the Islands.

In 1815–1816 came the Russian adventurer Scheffer, whose attempts to seize the island of Kaua'i were described in chapter 3. Starting in 1820, the year the American missionaries arrived, the United States and Britain began sending consuls and commercial agents to Hawai'i to increase their countries' influence there.

The French Catholic Mission

A new foreign influence appeared on the scene when a small French missionary group arrived in July 1827. Governor Boki, who had been baptized a Catholic in 1819, supported the priests. Ka'ahumanu opposed them, and tried to get them to leave.

In 1828, the Catholics lost the support of Boki, who died while in the South Pacific searching for sandalwood. After that began a period of persecution of Catholic converts and a campaign to expel their priests.

In 1831, two priests were forced to leave the islands, but other Catholics remained with the mission in Honolulu.

The treatment of the Catholics during this period can be explained in part. The American Mission did not want to share its ministry. The chiefs had been brought up to believe that worshipping the gods of a rival chief was wrong. They associated the Catholic converts with the policies of Boki and Liliha, who openly opposed the king. Also, they had never liked the French Catholic Jean Rives, who had

French priest Louis-Desire Maigret served the Sandwich Islands mission as bishop from 1847 until his death in 1882. Hawai'i State Archives

persecution: hurtful behavior toward a particular person or group

converts: those who have adopted a belief

expel: throw out; remove by force

Our Lady of Peace Cathedral, Honolulu, 1843. Hawai'i State Archives

strongly influenced Kamehameha II. To the older chiefs, the Catholics were a danger to the state.

Return of the Catholic Mission

By 1836, young Kamehameha III had taken personal control, with Kīna'u as *kuhina nui*. The Catholics tried again to set up a mission in Hawai'i. Kīna'u opposed the priests who arrived in the islands. The king was willing to let them stay if they preached only to European Catholics, not to Hawaiians.

At the end of the year, the king and chiefs issued severe rulings forbidding the teaching of Catholicism or the landing of priests. The persecution of Catholic Hawaiians began once more.

Kīna'u died in April 1839, and the king appointed Kekāuluohi, one of Liholiho's wives, to take her place. Now there was a better climate for religious toleration. In June, the king, influenced by William Richards, issued an order providing freedom of religion in the Islands.

Danger from France

The danger from France was not over. The French ministry was setting up colonies in the Pacific, especially in the Marquesas and Society Islands. In July 1839, French Captain Laplace dropped anchor in Honolulu harbor. His orders were to protect the rights of French nationals and of the Catholic religion, by force if necessary. Without making any real investigation and paying no attention to the king's new policy of toleration, he accused the chiefs of being misled by treacherous advisers. He then made a series of demands.

To enforce these demands, he kept the king's secretary onboard his frigate as hostage. He also declared a blockade and prepared to attack. In notes to the British and American consuls, he offered protection onboard the ship to their countrymen. He did not include the American missionaries. He said they were "the true authors of the insults offered to France" and were to be thought of as part of the local population.

The Hawaiian government was forced to yield. The *kuhina nui* and Governor Kekūanaō'a boarded the frigate with the desired treaty, signed on behalf of the king, and a

toleration: respect for the beliefs and acts of others

French flag

colonies: areas controlled by a far-off country

treacherous: not to be trusted

blockade: an action preventing ships from entering or leaving a harbor

82

$20,000 guarantee that the treaty would be kept. Two days later, when the king arrived from Maui, Laplace added more demands. No Frenchman was to be tried for any crime except by a jury of foreign residents chosen by the French consul. French wine and brandy were to be admitted with a duty of not more than five percent. He also demanded a site for a Catholic church and the release of all Catholic prisoners.

Later demands by French officials were met in one way or another, but France gained no permanent control.

The Paulet Episode

Now the British began to make demands and seek more control. Many foreign residents felt that annexation was in the air. This seems to have been the hope of the British consul, Richard Charlton.

The activities of Charlton were a prelude to the Paulet episode, a story that would furnish good material for a movie. Briefly, this is what happened:

The American firm of Ladd & Company signed a contract with the government in November 1841 leasing them valuable land for growing sugar. The company needed money from the king and from foreign investors to make the project work. To assure the foreign investors that their money would be safe, the company sent an employee to get guarantees of Hawaiian independence from England, France, and the United States.

In Honolulu, Sir George Simpson, governor in North America of the Hudson's Bay Company, told the chiefs that the Ladd & Company employee did not have enough authority to deal with foreign governments. He offered to form a commission to go to Washington. Other members of the commission were William Richards and Timothy Ha'alilio, a young Hawaiian who was secretary and confidant of the king.

The group sailed quietly in July 1842. As soon as Charlton learned about this, he sailed for London, hoping to defeat the move to recognize Hawaiian independence. Before leaving, he appointed Alexander Simpson, a cousin of Sir George Simpson, as acting consul. Alexander Simpson, unlike his cousin, openly favored annexation, and the king refused to accept him.

duty: a tax on imported goods

annexation: adding another area of land or political unit to one's own

prelude: something that leads to something else

episode: an event that is one of a series of related events

confidant: someone with whom private thoughts can be shared

British flag

Timothy Ha'alilio, a young Hawaiian, was a secretary and confidant to Kamehameha III. Hawai'i State Archives

Lord George Paulet demanded that Kamehameha III turn over the Hawaiian Islands to the English.
Guava Graphics

Dr. Gerrit Parmele Judd acted as an adviser to the government during the reign of Kamehameha III. During the Paulet episode, he advised Kamehameha to turn over the Islands to the British government temporarily to avoid a violent confrontation.
Guava Graphics

Richards and Ha'alilio reached Washington early in December. They presented their case for Hawai'i to President John Tyler and his cabinet so well that Secretary of State Daniel Webster gave them an official letter supporting the government of the Sandwich Islands.

Overjoyed at their success, Richards and Ha'alilio sailed in February 1843 to join Sir George Simpson in London. The British Foreign Secretary, Lord Aberdeen, supported them, saying that Great Britain should not become too powerful in the Islands.

Meanwhile, Consul Charlton and Alexander Simpson had both complained to Lord George Paulet, commander of the British frigate *Carysfort*, that British property rights were being violated. Admiral Richard Thomas, commander of British naval forces in the Pacific, sent Paulet to Hawai'i to investigate.

Upon arriving, Paulet demanded a private interview with the king. The king refused, saying that any private business could be discussed with Dr. G. P. Judd, adviser to the government. Paulet refused to deal with Judd, charging that he was the one behind the anti-British feeling. On February 17 he presented six demands related to the rights of the English in Hawai'i.

The king met several times with Paulet and Simpson, who made other demands. Dr. Judd advised the king not to resist but to turn over the Islands to the British government temporarily. He hoped that Richards and Ha'alilio would soon send help from London.

Kamehameha III and Kekāuluohi signed the document. The king issued a short announcement to his chiefs and his people:

> "Where are you, Chief, people and commons from my ancestor, and people from foreign lands!
>
> "Here ye! I make known to you that I am in perplexity by reason of difficulties into which I have been brought without cause; therefore, I have given away the life of our land, hear ye! But, my rule over you, my people, and your privileges will continue,

for I have hope that the life of the land will be restored when my conduct shall be justified." Sheldon Dibble, *A History of the Hawaiian Islands* (Honolulu: Thos. G. Thrum, 1919), p. 393.

The British now rapidly took over. Their flag went up and the Hawaiian flag came down. A commission, of which Dr. Judd was a member, was to run the government. Judd had no real power, however, and he soon resigned in disgust. All Hawaiian flags were destroyed. Government ships were put under British registry. Money was taken from the treasury to maintain a small army of Hawaiians called the Queen's Regiment. Various laws of the kingdom were changed at the will of the British commander. The king went to Lahaina.

Results of the Paulet Episode

Today it seems strange that a naval commander could act in this way. Communication was slow in those days, and naval officers had more authority in international relations than they do today. Besides, Paulet did not know that Lord Aberdeen supported Hawaiian independence.

Paulet was eager to report his actions to the British Foreign Office. As his messenger, he sent Alexander Simpson on a ship he had seized. The king and Judd knew they must get their story of what had happened to Washington and London as soon as possible. They also knew that Paulet would try to stop this if he knew about it.

It happened that the seized ship was under charter to Ladd & Company. The king and Judd decided to send the government's papers by the Ladd agent, James Marshall. Secretly they gave him formal papers addressed to the Queen of England and other documents prepared by Dr. Judd. Judd did his work in secret in the royal tomb, using the coffin of Kaʻahumanu as a desk. The king's signature was needed, so a canoe was sent to Maui for him. Slipping into Waikīkī at night, he signed the papers and returned to Maui.

Simpson and Marshall, who disliked each other intensely, set sail together in March. They parted in Mexico. Simpson raced for London and Marshall for Washington. After telling

99. Hawaiian Flag and Leis.

A flag-raising ceremony was held on July 31 after independence was restored to the Islands. Island Curio

British Rear Admiral Richard Thomas arrived to restore the independence of the Islands after the attempted takeover by Lord George Paulet.
Hawai'i State Archives

pavilions: temporary tents set up for special events

diplomat: a representative of one country who works directly with the government of another country

his story in Washington, Marshall joined Richards and Ha'alilio in London. There they prepared a reply to the accusations of Simpson and Charlton against the Hawaiian government.

Help for the Hawaiian government arrived on July 26. The news quickly spread that British Rear Admiral Richard Thomas had arrived to restore the independence of the Islands.

A flag-raising ceremony was held on July 31. The day dawned bright and clear. The entire population of Honolulu poured into a flat area east of town where pavilions and a flagstaff had been put up. A company of marines in dress uniform made a colorful formation. When the king and the admiral arrived, the king on horseback and the admiral riding in the king's carriage, a twenty-gun salute roared from the marines' field battery. The Hawaiian flag was raised, and a royal salute from the guns of the ships in port was answered by the guns at the fort and around the crest of Punchbowl. The Hawaiians later named the site of the ceremony "Thomas Square" in honor of the admiral. It is located on the present Beretania Street across from the Honolulu Academy of Arts.

Later, at Kawaiaha'o Church, the Hawaiian John 'Ī'ī gave a speech, and the king told his subjects that independence had been restored. He used words that became the motto of the State of Hawai'i. *U'u mau ke ea o ka 'āina i ka pono* ("The life of the land is preserved in righteousness").

For the next ten days the community celebrated. Judd recovered the state papers from the royal tomb and set the government in motion again. Meanwhile, across the sea, the British and French had signed a joint declaration that recognized the independence of the Sandwich Islands.

The United States showed that it recognized Hawai'i's growing importance by appointing a diplomatic representative rather than a consul.

In February 1844, a new British consul general, General William Miller, came to Honolulu to replace Charlton. He brought with him a treaty, which contained several objectionable articles. However, the king signed it in the hope that it would be improved. The French continued to act under the terms of the unsatisfactory treaty presented

The site of the flag-raising ceremony that restored Hawai'i's independence was later named "Thomas Square" after Rear Admiral Richard Thomas. Thomas Square is located between Beretania and King Streets, across from the Honolulu Academy of Arts. B. Bess

by Laplace. The United States made no formal treaty but declared once more that Hawai'i should be looked upon as an independent nation.

Reforms in Government

The Constitution of 1840 marked the change from an absolute to a constitutional monarchy. Like the American Constitution, it provided for a separation of powers. The executive power was in the hands of the king, the *kuhina nui*, and four governors. Laws were to be made by a two-house legislature. One branch, the House of Nobles, was to be made up of the king, the chiefs, and the *kuhina nui*. The other, the House of Representatives, would contain representatives chosen by the people. For the first time, male commoners could be part of the government. The judicial branch consisted of the king, the *kuhina nui*, and four judges chosen by the House of Representatives. Later laws set up five departments, each headed by a minister in the king's cabinet.

The next step was to modernize the framework of government and improve upon the Constitution of 1840. Dr. Judd, now the first secretary of state, began to gather around him men who could start the kingdom on its new course.

Robert C. Wyllie was Minister of Foreign Affairs and Secretary of War from 1845–1865. Wyllie served under Kamehameha III, IV, and V, and died while still in office. Guava Graphics

John Ricord, an adventurous young American lawyer, served for three years as attorney general. He performed a great service for Hawai'i's legal system and worked out a plan to modernize Hawai'i's government.

Robert C. Wyllie, a Scotsman, became minister of foreign affairs. William Richards became minister of public instruction after his return from Europe. John Young (Keoni Ana) served as prime minister and minister of the interior. He was the son of the John Young who had been a close adviser to Kamehameha I. Judd himself became minister of finance.

Lorrin Andrews from Maui was judge of cases involving foreigners. A newly arrived lawyer, William Lee, was widely respected for his calm good judgment. His eleven years of service were to be of great value to the kingdom. When the Organic Act of 1848 created a three-man superior court, Lee was appointed chief justice, with Andrews and John 'Ī'ī as associate justices.

As midcentury drew nearer, the missionaries held a leading place in the Hawaiian community. The foreign merchants and some of the leading Hawaiians charged them with liking money and power too much. Even the American Board at home criticized them for their political activities and their failure to train Hawaiians to take office. Catholics complained that their schools were not being treated fairly. The arrival of a Mormon mission in 1850 brought new complications. Dr. Judd was the target of many attacks, including some from the American commissioner and the British consul general.

New Troubles with France

New troubles with France arose in the spring of 1849. The French consul claimed French residents had been mistreated. He acted so badly that the government asked that he be returned to France. In August a French admiral arrived with two men-of-war. He backed up the consul and made a series of harsh demands on the Hawaiian government. These demands were met by a calm refusal.

French forces then landed and committed acts of vandalism. They occupied government buildings, dismantled the fort, seized the king's yacht, and destroyed furniture and

vandalism: purposeful destruction of public or private property

dismantled: tore apart

ornaments in the governor's house. When the Hawaiians watched their actions with curiosity rather than fear, the bewildered French set sail once more with the consul onboard.

The king and his council decided to send Dr. Judd and a special commission to France. The two young princes, Alexander Liholiho, who was heir to the throne, and his brother, Lot Kamehameha, went too. A large crowd cheered them as they began their journey in September 1849. They were greeted warmly in San Francisco and New York. In London their old friend Admiral Thomas entertained them. Everywhere on their travels in Europe the two princes were treated well. In Paris Judd could not get a stubborn ministry of foreign affairs to sign a new treaty, but the princes enjoyed their stay.

They were not so pleased with their experiences in the United States. In a handwritten journal now preserved in the Hawaiian Historical Society library, Prince Alexander Liholiho made an angry entry. His journal describes an incident in New York on June 5, 1850, as follows:

> While at the station waiting for the baggage to be checked, Mr. Judd told me to get in and secure seats. While I was sitting looking out of the window, a man came to me and told me to get out of the carriage . . . , saying that I was in the wrong carriage. I immediately asked him what he meant, he continued his request, finally he came around by the door, and I went out to meet him just as he was coming in. Somebody whispered a word in his ears. By this time I came up to him and asked him his reasons for telling me to get out of that carriage. He then told me to keep my seat. I took hold of his arm and asked him his reasons and what right he had in turning me out, and talking to me in the way that he did. He replied that he had some reasons, but requested me to keep my seat. And I followed him out, but he took care to be out of my way after that. I found he was the conductor,

Prince Liholiho was heir to the throne of Kamehameha III. Guava Graphics

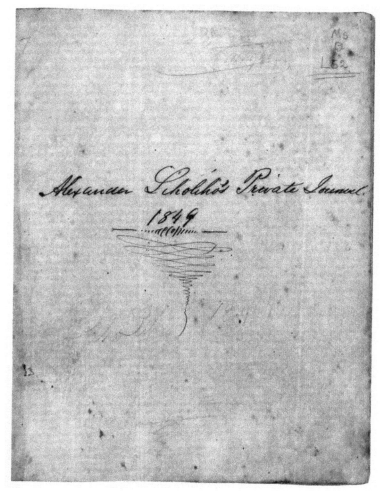

The journal of fifteen-year-old Alexander Liholiho is now preserved in the Hawaiian Historical Society library. Hawaiian Historical Society

and probably took me for somebody's servant just because I had a darker skin than he had. . . . The first time that I ever received such treatment—not in England, or France or anywhere else—but in this country, I must be treated like a dog, to go and come at an American's bidding. Here I must state that I am disappointed in the Americans.

Relations with the United States

Although Prince Alexander might be having his own personal troubles in the United States, relations between the two countries were improved by the visit of Dr. Judd. A treaty was signed in December 1849 that regulated relations between the two countries until Hawai'i was annexed to the United States.

After California was admitted to the Union in 1850, many Americans moved to Hawai'i. There were rumors that some adventurers from California planned to seize the Islands. A renewal of French claims brought new problems for the Hawaiian government. Some Americans in Hawai'i thought that the United States should act to prevent moves by France. The subject of annexation was introduced in the American Congress.

In the face of these difficulties, the king was persuaded to consider a treaty whereby the Islands would enter the American union as a state. The treaty was drafted by Wyllie and David Gregg, the new American commissioner, in the summer of 1854. For some months the matter dragged on. Finally it came to a halt with the death of the king on December 15.

But during all this period of trouble and uncertainty, one constructive action was taken. A new constitution for the Hawaiian kingdom was written.

Constitution of 1852

In 1851 three commissioners were appointed to draw up a new constitution. The king appointed Dr. Judd, the Nobles appointed Judge John 'Ī'ī, and the Representatives appointed Judge William L. Lee.

The new document, mainly the work of Judge Lee, was published in the *Polynesian* in November 1851. It was adopted by the legislature and sent to the king for his signature on June 14, 1852. The constitution provided for a two-house legislature. A House of Nobles, not to exceed thirty members, was to be appointed by the king for life. A House of Representatives, numbering not fewer than twenty-four or more than forty members, was to be elected annually. The privy council was now separated from the House of Nobles. The office of *kuhina nui* was continued.

privy council: group of advisers to the king

The king signed the new constitution to win the support and cooperation of foreigners. It gave more power to the Hawaiian people. But it also made changes to the people's relationship to the land (see chapter 9).

Summing Up the Chapter

A new influence came to the Islands with the arrival of the French Catholic Mission. For a time Governor Boki favored the mission, but Ka'ahumanu opposed the Catholics. After the death of Kīna'u in 1839, religious toleration increased. That same year the French Captain Laplace used force to make the Hawaiian government accept a treaty that contained outrageous demands. In 1843 Lord George Paulet, commander of a British frigate, forced the Hawaiian king to turn over his government to British control. The British government in London did not back up his move, and the Islands were again declared independent. By midcentury, efforts were being made in the Islands and in Washington to annex Hawai'i to the United States, but they were not successful. The new Constitution of 1852 gave more power to the Hawaiian people and to foreigners in Hawai'i.

Plantation workers came to the Islands to work in the sugar fields. Island Curio

9
Sugar and the Land

During the reign of Kamehameha III, the missionaries, the whalers and traders, and the politicians and lawyers were changing Hawai'i. Another revolution was also taking place: a revolution in agriculture. Its two most significant phases were growth of the sugar industry and the end of the traditional system of landholding.

revolution: complete change

Captain Cook noticed "spots of sugarcane on the higher ground" in the islands he visited. Apparently the Hawaiians did not try to make sugar from this cane. They merely chewed the soft stalks for the sweet sap inside. It would be many years before men would have the resources to produce the crop that would completely change the economy of the land.

It is not clear who made the first efforts to produce sugar commercially in the Islands. Some say a Chinese man tried to make sugar on the island of Lāna'i as early as 1802. He brought with him from China a crude mill of granite rollers and some pans for trying out the syrup, but his project failed. A Spaniard who settled on O'ahu experimented with sugar-making in 1819. Eight years later an Englishman tried to grow cane in Mānoa Valley.

The Founding of Kōloa Plantation

The first successful attempt in the sugar industry began in 1835. Three young New Englanders—Peter Brinsmade, William Ladd, and William Hooper—leased from Kamehameha III a 980-acre tract of land at Kōloa, Kaua'i. The lease was for fifty years at an annual rental of $300. It gave them a mill site, with a waterfall for power, and the right to build a road to the nearby landing. They later leased a warehouse site at the landing.

The young partners had come to Honolulu in 1833. Brinsmade and Ladd brought their wives, who were sisters. The men operated a successful business under the name of Ladd & Company. They decided to expand their business to include sugar. William Hooper agreed to manage the plantation, even though he had little experience in agriculture and could not speak Hawaiian.

They had many problems. Among other things, they needed more workers, more money to pay them, and better mill rollers. Still, at the end of the first year Hooper could write in his diary that he had over twenty thatched and adobe houses for his workers, a water-powered mill, twenty-five acres of cane, thousands of coffee and other trees, and forty-eight taro patches.

adobe: bricks made of clay and straw

Sugar Becomes King

Soon after Kōloa Plantation began operating, stone mills appeared on Maui, Hawai'i, and O'ahu. Some were run by Chinese. Some were simple ones operated by the mission stations for their own use. In the ten-year period following 1837, sugar production increased noticeably, although sales abroad were small. The California Gold Rush of 1849 caused a temporary boom, not only for sugar but also for other

94

Island crops. Another boom occurred at the beginning of the Civil War, when the Union blockade kept Louisiana sugar from reaching northern markets.

As the market grew, new improved mills appeared. More land was used for growing sugar, and the plantation became "big business." Owners began to join together to hire certain Honolulu commercial agencies, or factors, to buy their milling equipment, find markets, and handle financing.

factors: businesses that are paid to perform services for other businesses

The founder of the first factoring agency was James Hunnewell. In 1826 he started a store that later became C. Brewer & Company. Another agency was begun by a German sea captain named Hackfeld. His drygoods and general merchandise store, founded in 1849, later became American Factors. Another British firm, Starkey, Janion & Company started in 1845. By 1884, operating under the name of Theo. H. Davies & Company, it had also entered the sugar business. S. T. Alexander and H. P. Baldwin, sons of American missionaries, gave their names to still another successful sugar agency.

In 1837 Samuel Northrup Castle and Amos Starr Cooke, members of the eighth company of missionaries sent to Hawai'i by the American Board, reached Honolulu. Neither was a minister, but both took an active part in the work of the mission. In June 1851, they announced in the weekly *Polynesian* that they were going into business under the name of Castle and Cooke. This firm was the fifth of the "Big Five" factoring agencies, which still hold an important place in Hawai'i's business community.

By 1867 Castle and Cooke were servicing four sugar plantations on Maui, O'ahu, and Hawai'i. The one on Hawai'i was the Kohala Sugar Company, founded in 1863 by the Reverend Elias Bond. It is interesting to note his influence in some of the regulations drawn up for the guidance of plantation employees:

> "Said company shall not distill nor manufacture any spirituous liquors from the products of the Plantation.
>
> "The laborers and all belonging to the Plantation are requested to attend church once at least every Sunday.

Samuel Northrup Castle. Guava Graphics

Amos Starr Cooke. Guava Graphics

Samuel Northrup Castle and Amos Starr Cooke, two missionaries, opened a sugar manufacturing business under the name Castle and Cooke. This firm was the fifth of the "Big Five" sugar factoring agencies.

Benjamin Dillingham came to Honolulu as a sailor in 1865. He decided to stay and eventually began the Oʻahu Railway and Land Company.
Guava Graphics

Captain William Matson started a steamship line to take sugar and other island products to the United States.
Guava Graphics

epidemics: diseases spreading rapidly and infecting many people at one time

"There is to be no card playing.

"No fighting is allowed under penalty of one dollar for each offense; the money is to be laid out on Books and Papers.

"No quarreling with or whipping wives is allowed under penalty of one dollar for each offense.

"No tittle tattling is allowed, or gossiping." Castle and Cooke, *The First 100 Years* (Honolulu, 1951), p. 18.

Other companies sprang up to service the young sugar industry. For repairing milling machinery, Theophilus H. Davies helped to finance the Honolulu Iron Works Company in 1875. A cabinetmaker named Christopher Lewers opened a shop that supplied construction material. Out of it has come Lewers and Cooke, Ltd., one of Hawaiʻi's most important construction firms. Benjamin Dillingham, a sailor, married a missionary's daughter, went into the railroad business, and built a sugar warehouse. Captain William Matson started a steamship line to take sugar and other island products to the United States. James Campbell tried his fortunes on Maui and later founded the Pioneer Mill Plantation. Waldemar Knudsen, son of a noted Norwegian, came to Hawaiʻi by way of California after a series of misfortunes and won success as a sugar planter. Paul Isenberg, a German immigrant, became a noted sugar proprietor on Kauaʻi.

Ambitious foreigners were seeking their fortunes, and in doing so they were building a new community in the Pacific.

Solving the Labor Shortage

By midcentury, new sources of labor were needed. Thousands of Hawaiians had died during epidemics. Irrigation and improved growing methods made it possible for planters to plant more sugarcane and produce more sugar, but workers were not available to take care of the crops.

In 1850 the newly organized Royal Hawaiian Agricultural Society, a group of residents interested in improving marketing and crop control, discussed ways of importing workers from abroad. They made a contract with the captain of a British ship to bring laborers from South China ports. In January 1852, about two hundred of them arrived, followed by one hundred more in August. They were brought in under a contract labor system, which paid them three dollars a month for five years. Transportation, food, clothing, and housing were also provided. The Masters' and Servants' Act of 1850 set penalties for workers who broke their contracts, and for planters who treated the workers cruelly or unfairly.

A steady stream of Chinese entered the Islands until the end of the century. Many of them paid their own way, and many went back to China after they had served the term of their contract. Most were good plantation workers. As time went on, many began to leave the canefields for the towns, especially Honolulu, where they got into the retail trade and truck gardening.

truck gardening: growing vegetables to sell

During the second half of the nineteenth century the lack of field workers continued to be a problem. The government encouraged the immigration of contract laborers from countries other than China. The effects of this policy are discussed in later chapters.

The Mahele

For successful sugar planting, capital, labor, and land are necessary. The land was there, but how were the planters to get title to it?

title: legal ownership

Before the coming of foreigners, landholding was managed under a system in which the king and the high chiefs controlled the land, which was managed by the *konohiki*. In return the people gave the chiefs part of what they produced.

Many Hawaiians thought the people were better off with the old system. They thought the land belonged to the gods and that the chiefs knew best how to control its use. But most westerners did not understand the relationship Hawaiians had with the land. They thought the people should have the right to own their own land and pass that land on to their children. As early as 1825, a council of chiefs passed laws allowing children of chiefs to inherit land. These laws made the position of the chiefs more secure. It did not, however, help the commoners or the foreigners.

By the time Kamehameha III came to the throne, more and more foreigners were demanding ownership of the land with a clear title. This led to the passage of the Bill of Rights of 1839. It stated that land could not be taken from the people except by due process of law. The constitution of 1840 went on to say that the land was not the private property of the king, but was owned in common with chiefs and people under the management of the king. The common people could not obtain absolute ownership, but they could not be forced off their land without the use of legal means.

tenants: those who pay to use or live on land owned by someone else

The Constitution of 1840 defined a number of rights and privileges of landowners and tenants. However, it did little to assure foreigners that they could legally own the property in which they had invested money. The problem became so serious that in December 1845 a board was created with the title "Commissioners to Quiet Land Titles." These commissioners were to decide the rights and interests of all people, including foreigners, who had claims on land before 1845. They had full power to decide these claims. A law passed in 1850 gave foreigners the right to own land.

The job of the commissioners was a very difficult one. To judge fairly, the commission had to consider overlapping interests among people who did not understand the principle of individual ownership. Many people did not apply for title to their land. Others quickly sold their holdings without realizing their value. The actual surveying of the land was a problem because there were few qualified surveyors in the kingdom. Some of the missionaries offered to help with the surveying and to persuade people to apply for titles to their land.

surveying: determining the boundaries of a piece of land

After the appointment of the land commission, the next step was to decide the rights of the king, the chiefs, and the *konohiki* in the various undivided portions of the land. A committee set up guidelines for the division of lands within the kingdom. Their proposals were as follows:

1. The king kept all his private lands. Tenants of that land could own one-third of the land they farmed.
2. One-third of the remaining lands went to the Hawaiian government; one-third went to the chiefs and *konohiki*. One-third went to the commoners who worked on the

land. This division would take place whenever any of the parties asked for it.

3. The division would not affect any lands that the king or one of the earlier kings had already granted to any Hawaiian subject or foreigner.

4. To cover the costs of the transfer, the chiefs and *konohiki* could either give one-third of their lands to the government or pay a sum equal to one-third of the unimproved value of their lands.

Each *mahele* was a signed agreement between the king and a chief or a *konohiki*, transferring land to them. The first was signed in January 1848, and the job was completed about six weeks later. The individual divisions were written down in a large book, the *Mahele Book*. After a division was agreed upon, a chief presented his claim before the land commission and received an award for the lands. After he paid the commission fee, he received a Royal Patent.

Now a further division of land was made between the king and the government. The king set aside the larger part of his lands for the benefit of the government and kept other lands for himself and his heirs. The part that he kept became known as "crown lands." Kamehameha III and his successors sold, leased, and mortgaged these lands at will until 1865. In that year a law was passed declaring that crown lands should not pass out of the hands of the king and his heirs. When the monarchy was overthrown in 1893, the remaining crown lands were seized and became public lands.

The last step in the Mahele had to do with the rights of the Hawaiian tenants, wherever they lived. An act passed in August 1850 provided for titles for Hawaiian tenants. To get these titles they had to prove that they actually improved the land they lived on and depended on it for their living. These lands were known as *kuleana* lands.

The *kuleana* lands were mostly taro lots, much more valuable than the waste or forest land that was a large part of the area assigned to the king and the chiefs. But many commoners did not do the things they needed to do to claim their *kuleana*. They ended up with only one percent of the available land. Later, some lost their *kuleana* because they

Taro patch. B. Bess

mahele: division

mortgaged: offered in payment for debts

kuleana: responsibility, right, or ownership

did not pay land taxes or because they did not continue to live on the land. When that happened, foreigners bought and sold the *kuleana*. Thus one of the purposes of Kamehameha III in his support of the Mahele—to settle commoners on their own land—was in part defeated.

Summing Up the Chapter

Little was done to develop the sugar industry until 1835, when Kōloa Plantation was founded. Sugar mills appeared all over the Islands. Factoring agencies were formed to handle the buying, marketing, and financing of groups of sugar plantation owners. Because of a labor shortage in the Islands, workers had to be imported from abroad. Foreigners did not like the old system of landholding. Under Kamehameha III and later rulers, laws were passed that divided the land and gave clear legal titles to the owners. For various reasons many of the Hawaiians did not keep the lands assigned to them.

10
Shifting Influences and King Kamehameha IV (1854–1863)

Kamehameha III's nephew, Alexander Liholiho, was named Kamehameha IV. Kawaiaha'o Church

View of Smallpox Hospital, Paul Emmert. Hawaiian Historical Society

Worn out physically and wearied by the many dangers that threatened his country, King Kamehameha III died on December 16, 1854, after an illness of five or six days.

The Smallpox Plague

One event that darkened the last years of Kamehameha III's reign was the outbreak of smallpox in the Islands. In February 1853, a ship arrived from San Francisco, where the disease was common. The ship flew a yellow flag on the foremast, a sign that there was smallpox aboard.

Upon arrival, the crew was quarantined and watched closely. The sick man was put in a separate house. The

quarantined: kept away from others to prevent the spread of disease ship was quarantined for twenty-one days, and all bedding was burned. Eventually the man recovered and the vessel departed.

In May two women in Honolulu came down with the disease. They probably became infected from laundering the clothing of seamen who had been exposed to smallpox in San Francisco.

Attempts to prevent the spread of smallpox failed. Panic swept over the community, especially in Honolulu and the 'Ewa district, where the disease was most severe. Three commissioners of public health were given full power to make rules that might stop the spread of the disease.

They set up temporary hospitals and limited travel between the islands. Frantic efforts were made to vaccinate the people. After August the disease was not so severe. Whaling ships arrived in September, with crews of two or three thousand, most of whom had not been vaccinated. They were kept onboard until doctors were able to vaccinate them. Only one foreigner died of smallpox. Deaths among the local population, however, were very high. The commissioners of public health estimated the number of cases at 6,405, of whom 2,485 died.

vaccinate: to protect from disease by injecting with a very weak form of the disease bacteria or virus

Moves Toward Annexation

Another problem that faced the king came from the growing number of Americans living in the Islands. By midcentury, the United States was interested in expansion. It owned rich new lands in Oregon and Washington. The war with Mexico had given the United States most of the remaining lands of the West. The Gold Rush had brought thousands of Americans to the West Coast. Now there were exciting prospects of trade with the Far East. Hawai'i was an attractive steppingstone on the long journey to Japan and China. Americans claimed that foreign nations, especially France, threatened the monarchy. For these and other reasons, they wanted the United States to annex Hawai'i.

expansion: growing larger by adding new land

The British and French representatives were against annexation, while a local "Committee of Thirteen" was in favor of it. In the U.S. Congress there were speeches in favor of making the Islands a part of the Union. American newspapers also supported the movement.

Meanwhile, American commissioner David L. Gregg and Robert Wyllie were discussing an annexation agreement. Prince Alexander Liholiho, the king's heir, believed that Hawai'i did not need or want annexation.

In November came the report that adventurers were coming from California to overthrow the government by force. Commanders of British, French, and American warships at Honolulu Harbor promised Wyllie that they would protect the Hawaiian government from any such attempt. The prince and Wyllie were now sure that annexation would not become necessary.

When the king died a few weeks later, all talks were broken off. The proposed treaty would probably not have been approved by the U.S. Senate, since the United States had already agreed to respect Hawai'i's independence. The threat of annexation had passed, but it would arise again.

The New King

Alexander Liholiho, who became Kamehameha IV, was born in 1834. He was the son of Kīna'u and Governor Kekūanō'a of O'ahu. Liholiho's rank as high chief came from Kīna'u, who was the daughter of Kamehameha I and the half-sister of both Kamehameha II and Kamehameha III. Since Kamehameha III did not have any children, he took Liholiho, his nephew, as his *hānai* son and heir.

In the same edition of *The Friend* that described the death of Kamehameha III, the editor wrote of Alexander:

> He was educated at the Royal School, when under the charge of Mr. A. S. Cooke. As a scholar he exhibited many good qualities. At the examinations of that school, he always appeared well versed in the ordinary branches of a good English education. In bookkeeping, surveying, and arithmetic, he exhibited a more than ordinary acquaintance, as we are able to testify from our own personal recollection. . . . During the last three or four years, he has been, more or less, actively engaged in the affairs of the government. He has been at the head of the military

STONE CHURCH AT HONOLULU.

Kawaiaha'o Church was built in 1846. Hawai'i State Archives

Kawaiaha'o Church today. B. Bess

In 1856, Alexander Liholiho married Emma Rooke, a granddaughter of John Young, a trusted adviser of Kamehameha I. Young Emma is pictured here between her parents, Dr. and Mrs. T. C. B. Rooke. Hawai'i State Archives

department of the kingdom, and an active member of the House of Nobles. As a member of that body, he has often exhibited an ability, as a parliamentary debator, which would have done credit to a person of more years and greater experience.

In 1856, the young king married Emma Rooke, a granddaughter of John Young, the trusted adviser of Kamehameha I. In childhood she had been adopted by Dr. T. C. B. Rooke, an English physician who had married Emma's aunt.

The wedding took place at Kawaiaha'o Church, with the Reverend Richard Armstrong officiating. The king, as nervous as any other bridegroom, forgot the ring. A government official solved the problem by pulling a ring from his finger and offering it to the king. Thousands of Hawaiians gathered

Kawaiaha'o Church, where Alexander Liholiho and Queen Emma were married. B. Bess

on the church grounds to honor the young couple. One of the bridesmaids was Victoria Lydia Paki, who was later to become Queen Lili'uokalani.

Two years later the queen gave birth to a son, whom she and the king named Albert. The Hawaiians were happy that the Kamehameha line would continue. The privy council gave the child the title of "His Royal Highness the Prince of Hawai'i" (*Ka Haku o Hawai'i*). In 1859 he was officially named the heir of Kamehameha IV.

Decline of the Hawaiian Population

In his first message to the legislature in 1855, the king called attention to the terrible decrease of the Hawaiian population. He recommended building public hospitals and trying to prevent the spread of foreigners' diseases. Money was voted for this purpose, but it was not used.

The king and queen continued to press for hospitals for sick and penniless Hawaiians. Finally, in 1859, the legislature approved the collection of funds. Immediately the royal couple went into the community asking for money for a hospital. In the spring of 1860, a board of trustees bought land at the corner of Beretania and Punchbowl Streets. By the end of the next year, a permanent two-story building had been built and named Queen's Hospital. Dr. William Hillebrand was put in charge of the hospital, and money was voted by the legislature to maintain it.

At first the people did not want to use the new hospital. They were used to the services of their *kahuna* and had little faith in the *haole* doctors. As time passed, they began to come for treatment and prescriptions.

The Queen's Medical Center, located today on the same site as the old building, honors the memory of Kamehameha IV and his queen.

Foreign Relations

reciprocity: an equal exchange; giving and getting the same thing in return

One of the most important aims of Kamehameha IV was a reciprocity treaty with the United States. The treaty would allow Hawaiian and American goods to be exchanged without the payment of duty. He thought that such a treaty might remove the threat of annexation and do away with the fears of the American sugar planters. It would create a much

Queen Emma and King Kamehameha IV worked to create support for hospitals for the poor. In 1861, a permanent two-story building was built and named Queen's Hospital. The Queen's Medical Center, located today on the same site as the old building, honors the memory of Queen Emma and Kamehameha IV. Hawai'i State Archives

larger market for Hawaiian sugar, and the whole economy of the Islands would benefit.

In 1855 Chief Justice William L. Lee persuaded President Franklin Pierce and Secretary of State William L. Marcy to sign a treaty. It was also approved by the Hawaiian government, but not the American Senate. Southern sugar planters and western wool producers opposed the treaty and were strong enough to keep it from being approved.

Another problem in foreign relations had to do with the treaty that had been made with France in 1846. The Hawaiians wanted a treaty more like those they had signed with the United States and Great Britain. They objected to the low import tax on French brandy and to the right of Frenchmen to be tried by a jury picked by the French consul. The French, on the other hand, complained that Catholics were being oppressed in Hawai'i and that official

The Queen's Medical Center today.
B. Bess

documents could be written only in the English and Hawaiian languages.

Finally, a new treaty was drawn up. The king was not completely satisfied with it, but he wanted to stay on friendly terms with the French and approved it in September 1858.

The Anglican Church

In that same year an interesting religious debate took place in Honolulu. A number of people had been members of the Church of England or of the Protestant Episcopal Church in America. They wanted to bring up their children in that faith. The king and the queen warmly supported the project. Minister Wyllie also favored having an Episcopal Church in the Islands. The American missionaries were against the move. They feared that this would bring about a union of church and state. They also feared that British influence would become too powerful and their own work would be forgotten or valued less.

Nevertheless, the king went ahead with the project, partly because of remorse over something that he did in September 1859. While on a trip to Maui, the king became jealous over a rumor about his friend and private secretary, Henry Neilson, and the queen. The king, after drinking heavily, shot Neilson. It was later proved that Neilson was innocent of the charges. Neilson, who was an invalid until he died in 1862, forgave the king, but the king could not forgive himself. He even thought of giving up the throne but was kept from this by his advisers and by public opinion. He tried to find peace in religion and continued to encourage the Episcopalians to come to Hawai'i.

The king offered land for a church. He also personally asked Queen Victoria of England for support. In 1861 Dr. Thomas N. Staley was sent from England to become the bishop of what was to be the Anglican Church in Hawai'i.

Queen Victoria had agreed to be godmother to little Prince Albert of Hawai'i. The wife of the new British consul-general in Hawai'i was to represent her at the prince's baptism, conducted by Bishop Staley. But on October 1, 1862, before the bishop reached Honolulu, a terrible thing happened. The little prince died after a short illness.

remorse: sorrow and shame

invalid: someone who suffers constantly from being ill or disabled

Prince Albert of Hawai'i became ill and died before he was to be baptized in the Anglican church. Guava Graphics

A few weeks after the bishop's arrival, the royal couple and several high-ranking officials became members of the church. At first the services were held in a building on Nuʻunau Street. Later a church was built on the site of the present St. Andrew's Cathedral.

The first Anglican church in Honolulu was built on the site where St. Andrew's Cathedral stands today. RJBest, Inc.

The Hawaiian Evangelical Association

In 1863 the American Protestant mission in Hawaiʻi was cut loose from its parent organization, the American Board of Commissioners for Foreign Missions. The time had come for the American missionaries to handle their own affairs, to train Hawaiian pastors, and to reorganize parishes. The Hawaiian Evangelical Association, formed in 1854, was now reorganized and took over the duties of the American Board.

The Mormon Movement

Another important religious development was the Mormon movement in Hawaiʻi, which had begun in 1850. After some success, especially on the island of Lānaʻi, the Mormon missionaries were called back to Salt Lake City by Brigham Young, the leader of Mormons in America. This left the mission without leadership. Into this situation stepped

Walter Murray Gibson was the leader of Mormons in Hawai'i. Guava Graphics

The Mormon temple at Lā'ie on O'ahu was built in 1919 on land purchased by Mormon missionaries in 1865. B. Bess

excommunicated: not allowed to remain a member of a church

Walter Murray Gibson, who arrived in Honolulu in the summer of 1861.

Gibson was the son of English emigrants to the United States. After living in New York, Central America, California, and the East Indies, he visited Salt Lake City. Here he met Brigham Young and was baptized into the Mormon faith. As a missionary, he found his way to Hawai'i, with his daughter Talula. He quickly became the leader of the Mormons in Hawai'i. Gibson raised money to buy the lands on Lāna'i that had been leased by the Mormon community on that island. There he made his home.

By 1864, some of Gibson's activities caused Brigham Young to send an investigating group to Hawai'i. They found that Gibson himself had the title to the lands on Lāna'i, which had been bought with church funds. For this and for other questionable activities, he was excommunicated, and most of his followers left the island. Gibson kept the land, which he turned into a sheep ranch. Later, he was to hold a key position in the political affairs of the Islands.

In 1865, the Mormon mission bought lands at Lā'ie on the island of O'ahu. The mission grew steadily until today the Mormons occupy a strong and respected position in business, church, and educational circles in Hawai'i.

The Civil War and Hawai'i

On May 9, 1861, the *Pacific Commercial Advertiser* told the people of Honolulu that a great civil war had broken out in the United States. Its startling headlines read, "War! Attack on Fort Sumter by the Confederate Army! Unconditional Surrender by Major Anderson!"

Even though Hawai'i's American residents sympathized with the North, the government declared itself neutral.

The effects of the war in Hawai'i were mainly economic. The whaling industry was already showing signs of decline. Now whaling ships were pressed into wartime service or laid up for the rest of the war. Many whalers were sunk by confederate privateers. A few Island residents joined the Union forces. The sugar industry boomed because of heavy demands and higher prices. A number of new plantations were started.

Finally the war ended, and, on May 13, 1865, the *Advertiser* reported the sad news of Abraham Lincoln's assassination. The June 1 issue of *The Friend* appeared with heavy black columns containing a long sermon by the editor on the death of the President.

Summing Up the Chapter

The last years of the reign of Kamehameha III were darkened by a smallpox epidemic, which killed many Hawaiians. The king sent commissioners to the United States to try to have the Islands annexed to the United States. They were not successful. The new king, Kamehameha IV, married soon after he took the throne. His only son and heir died while still a small boy. The king and queen took the lead in setting up a hospital that would serve the poor. A new treaty was made with France, but Hawai'i failed to get a free-trade treaty with the United States. During this time, the Episcopal Church came to Hawai'i, the American missions separated from their home board, and the Mormon missionaries arrived. The American Civil War hurt the whaling industry but helped the sugar planters.

A letter from President Abraham Lincoln to Kamehameha IV, dated March 16, 1863, informing him of the appointment of James McBride as the Minister Resident of the United States to Hawai'i. In this letter, Lincoln addresses Kamehameha as his "Great and Good Friend," and says of Mr. McBride's appointment, "I therefore request Your Majesty to receive him favorably and to give full credence to whatever he shall say to you on the part of the United States, and most of all when he shall assure you of their friendship and wishes for the prosperity of Your Kingdom." Signed, "Your Good Friend, Abraham Lincoln."
Hawai'i State Archives

neutral: not taking either side

11
Kamehameha V:
The Kamehameha
Dynasty Ends
(1863–1872)

Upon Kamehameha IV's death on November 30, 1863, Prince Lot Kamehameha was declared King Kamehameha V.
Kawaiaha'o Church

Midway during the U.S. Civil War, on November 30, 1863, King Kamehameha IV died, at the age of twenty-nine. Prince Lot Kamehameha was declared King Kamehameha V by his sister, Victoria Kamāmalu, the *kuhina nui*.

The New King

Lot Kamehameha was the older brother of Kamehameha IV. Like his younger brother he had been well educated at the Chief's Children's School and had traveled widely. He had held many positions of trust in the government. During Alexander's reign, he had been commander of the army, minister of the interior, and head of the finance department. During his reign he entered personally into all important discussions and selected ministers who supported his ideas. Some of his acts were strongly attacked, but he believed that his policies were for the good of Hawai'i.

He believed the king's right, going back to his grandfather, Kamehameha I, was to lead the people firmly. At his inauguration, he refused to take the oath to support the Constitution of 1852. Because he thought his people needed to be protected from waste and idleness, he refused to repeal the law against selling liquor to Hawaiians. He required people to be educated and to own property before they could vote.

repeal: cancel

While Lot may have been tough with his people, he was equally hard on the *haole*. Lot meant to be a ruling monarch and did not care much what *haole* thought of him. The Americans, especially, did not care for Lot. In the legislature, *haole* members refused to learn Hawaiian, and Hawaiian representatives refused to speak English. The fact that anything at all got done there was due largely to the interpreter, William Ragsdale, who was half-Hawaiian and half-*haole*. Mark Twain, who visited Hawai'i during Lot's reign, said of Ragsdale:

> Bill Ragsdale stands up in front of the Speaker's pulpit, with his back against it, and fastens his quick black eye upon any member who rises, lets him say half a dozen

kanaka: Hawaiian word for "person," used here to mean "Hawaiian language"

felicity: pleasantness of sound or style

republic: a government run by representatives elected by the people

literacy: ability to read and write

sentences and then interrupts him, and repeats his speech in a loud, rapid voice, turning every Kanaka speech into English and every English speech into Kanaka, with a readiness and felicity of language that are remarkable—waits for another installment of talk from the member's lips and goes on with his translation as before. His tongue is in constant motion from eleven in the forenoon till four in the afternoon, and why it does not wear out is the affair of Providence, not mine.

Lot disliked Americans because he feared that Hawai'i would become a republic like the United States and be annexed by that country. With this in mind, he forced upon his people a new constitution limiting the rights of his kingdom.

The Constitution of 1864

As an *ali'i,* Kamehameha V believed that he should be firmly in control of the government. Like his brother, he often did not like the controls put upon him by the Constitution of 1852. Instead of taking an oath to support the existing constitution, he called for a convention to draw up a new constitution.

In order to explain the proposed changes to his people, the king traveled to the other islands. Upon his return, he met with his advisers, especially Wyllie and Attorney General Charles Harris. Carefully he wrote the draft of a new constitution, which he presented to the convention at Kawaiaha'o Church.

The members of the convention could not agree, especially on the question of voting rights. Impatient, the king ended the meeting and announced that his constitution would be the law of the land.

The Constitution of 1864 abolished the old office of *kuhina nui*. It increased the power of the king and his cabinet. It combined the House of Representatives and the House of Nobles into one legislature. Voters born after 1840 had to pass a literacy test, and both voters and representatives had to own a certain amount of property. In spite of the way it was forced on the kingdom, the constitution lasted for the next twenty-three years.

Problems of Immigration

Soon after Kamehameha V came to the throne, he began to study the problem of finding workers for the sugar plantations. Early in 1864 a "Planters' Society" had been formed to deal with the problem. One of the leaders was Minister Wyllie. As owner of the Princeville Plantation on Kaua'i, he had a personal interest in the matter. The king asked some of his ministers to meet with the society to find ways to obtain a fresh labor supply.

As a result of this conference, a Bureau of Immigration was to regulate and encourage the flow of immigration to the Islands. Commissioners were sent abroad to find workers. In 1868 the first group of Japanese was brought to Hawai'i under a three-year contract. They were paid four dollars per month. Two hundred more Japanese came in

The Bureau of Immigration regulated and increased the flow of immigrants to the islands in response to a labor shortage on Hawai'i's sugar plantations. Hawai'i State Archives

Immigrants from all over the world came to Hawai'i to work in the plantation fields. Hawai'i State Archives

1885. After that the Japanese arrived steadily until 1908. Large numbers of Portuguese, mostly from the island of Madeira, began to arrive in 1878. A small number of Norwegians and Germans came also. Beginning in 1906, many Filipinos entered Hawai'i.

These contract workers from China, Japan, and other countries partly met the needs of the planters. However, some people in Hawai'i, the United States, and Great Britain compared the contract labor system to the slave system in the United States. In 1872 the legislature passed several acts to protect the rights of the workers. The labor supply and immigration, however, remained problems for the successors of Kamehameha V.

Father Damien's Home, Molokai Hawaiian Islands. 126.

During the 1860s, leprosy became a dangerous threat to the people of Hawai'i. Those who were infected with the disease were sent to an isolated part of Moloka'i called Kalaupapa. Island Curio

Hansen's Disease in Hawai'i

A new threat to the health of Hawai'i's people came in the 1860s. Leprosy, today called "Hansen's disease," was known in Hawai'i as the *mai Pāke* (Chinese disease), because it was mistakenly thought to have been brought from China. There had been some cases before the reign of Kamehameha IV, but by 1865 it had become such a threat that the legislature took steps to handle it. So they would not infect others, those with the disease were sent to an isolated part of the island of Moloka'i. There, on a peninsula separated from the rest of the island by rugged cliffs, a colony was started in 1866.

Foreign Relations

The outbreak of the U.S. Civil War affected Hawaiian foreign relations. Hawai'i declared itself neutral in 1861, and the United States accepted this. However, several factors, including the pro-British monarchy, the introduction of the Anglican Church by Kamehameha IV, and the repeal of the Constitution of 1852 by Kamehameha V, cooled the relations between Hawai'i and the United States. Nevertheless, in 1863 the United States raised the status of its representative in Hawai'i to "minister resident." This was the highest

174 CULTIVATING RICE FIELD WITH WATER BUFFALOES, HAWAIIAN ISLANDS.

Livestock became an increasingly important labor and food source in the nineteenth century. Island Curio

diplomatic rank of all countries having representatives in Honolulu at that time.

Economics

Kamehameha V's time saw radical changes in the economic life of Hawai'i. Whaling declined and lost its place to sugar as the main industry in the Islands. A severe economic depression occurred as a result of the whaling disaster of 1871, when thirty-three vessels that had been regularly expected in the islands were trapped in ice elsewhere. Cargoes were abandoned and lost.

As whaling died, sugar rose. Steam machinery was introduced on sugar plantations, and production increased, even though the United States failed to sign a treaty allowing sugar into American ports duty free.

The Civil War caused sugar prices to rise and encouraged sugar planting in Hawai'i. In 1865 the exportation of sugar was ten times what it had been in 1860. This expansion was too fast and was based largely on borrowed money. When the war ended, prices dropped. A number of plantations did not have enough money to stay in business. By 1871, however, sugar exports reached a new high of ten thousand tons. But production slowed again, and the period from 1872 to 1873 was a time of depression.

Rice and coffee were also important crops. Ranches were

successful raising livestock. Lot, as a prince, had been the first president of a Grazier's Association organized in 1856 on Oʻahu.

grazier: a person who raises cattle

Another product grown at this time was *pulu*, which was exported to California between 1851 and 1884.

pulu: a silky or wooly fiber that grows at the base of tree fern fronds; it was used as a filling for mattresses and pillows.

All of these important changes in the economy increased the need for better means of transportation among the islands and between Hawaiʻi and her foreign markets.

Transportation and Commerce

During the reign of Kamehameha V (1863–1872) several important advances in transportation were made. American interest in the Pacific and the Far East led to steamer transportation between Honolulu and San Francisco and between Honolulu and Australia. Completion of the Pacific railroad across the United States in 1869 also brought people to Hawaiʻi. With steamers bringing more travelers to the

Richards and Hotel Streets today.
B. Bess

With steamers bringing more travelers to the islands than ever before, Honolulu needed more hotels to accommodate visitors. During 1871–72, the government built the Hawaiian Hotel at the corner of Richards and Hotel Streets. Island Curio

islands than ever before, Honolulu needed more and better hotels. During 1871–72 the government built the Hawaiian Hotel at the corner of Richards and Hotel Streets for over $110,000. Unfortunately, this construction doubled the national debt and led to the political downfall of two cabinet ministers who had promoted the project.

Lot's sister, Princess Victoria
Kamāmalu, was chosen to succeed
him. Unfortunately, she died in 1866,
six years before the king.
Kawaiahaʻo Church

The End of the Kamehameha Dynasty

Since Lot was a bachelor, his sister, Princess Victoria Kamāmalu, was named his successor by the Constitution of 1864. Unfortunately, she died in 1866. When the king died, on December 11, 1872, his fortieth birthday, he left no heir.

Summing Up the Chapter

With the death of Kamehameha IV, his elder brother became Kamehameha V. Lot's Constitution of 1864 gave more power to the king and to those with education and land. The Bureau of Immigration was formed to find people to come to work in the Islands. By the 1860s Hansen's disease had become a threat in the Islands. A colony for patients was set up on Molokaʻi in 1866. The policies of Lot Kamehameha were similar to those of Alexander. The main problems involved foreign relations, particularly with the United States. American-born sugar planters hoped Hawaiʻi would be annexed to the United States so that they could avoid heavy import duties. The government sought, instead, a treaty that would allow Hawaiian and American products to be exchanged duty free. With the advance of sugar and other forms of agriculture came an advance in transportation methods, the opening of new trade routes, and tourism.

12
Lunalilo,
the People's Choice
(1873–1874)

Lunalilo, Kamehameha I's grandnephew, was voted the new king by the people of Hawai'i. Popular with all classes of people, he was affectionately referred to as "the people's prince." Kawaiaha'o Church

High Chiefess Bernice Pauahi Bishop, the last descendant of Kamehameha I, declined when King Lunalilo asked her to succeed him. Kawaiaha'o Church

David Kalākaua lost to Lunalilo in the election to choose a successor to Kamehameha V. Guava Graphics

circular: a notice given out to large numbers of people

As Kamehameha V lay dying on December 11, 1872, he called the High Chiefess Bernice Pauahi (Mrs. Charles R. Bishop) to his bedside and asked her to be his successor. Although she was the last living descendant of Kamehameha I, she refused to accept the offer.

This was the first time the country had been left without a ruler. The American minister to Hawai'i, Henry A. Peirce, and the British representative, Theo. H. Davies, feared rioting and bloodshed. Each asked his government to send a warship to Hawai'i to help keep the peace.

Candidates for the Throne

Since Kamehameha V died without naming a successor, the legislature had to decide who would be king. The leading candidates for the throne were William C. Lunalilo, the highest-ranking chief, and David Kalākaua, also a high chief. Of the two, Lunalilo, who was Kamehameha I's grandnephew (his grandfather was Kamehameha's half-brother), was more popular with all classes of people. He was, in fact, called "the people's prince."

Six days after the death of the king, Lunalilo announced that he wanted the people to decide who would be king. He wanted every man in the kingdom to take part in an election. He promised to change the constitution and to give the people a greater voice in the government.

The election was unofficial, since only the legislature had the right to decide who would be king. Nevertheless, everyone thought the legislature would follow the wishes of the people.

Before the election, a group calling itself the "Skillful Genealogists" secretly published a circular that attacked Lunalilo's claim to be descended from Kamehameha's half-brother. This attack angered Lunalilo's supporters and made them work harder.

A few days later Kalākaua published his own proclamation. It said, in part:

> Let me direct you, my people! Do nothing contrary to the law or against the peace of the Kingdom. Do not go and vote.

Do not be led by foreigners; they had no
part in our hardships, in gaining the country.
Do not be led by their false teachings.

Kalākaua promised to bring back the Law of the Splintered Paddle, repeal all personal taxes, put Hawaiians into the national government, and change the Constitution of 1864. Kalākaua thought foreigners influenced Lunalilo too much. The struggle for the crown clearly showed the differences between the two men.

The Election of Lunalilo

Kalākaua's words had little effect on the voters. On New Year's Day, 1873, Lunalilo easily won a popular election. But would the legislature follow the wishes of the people? Lunalilo's supporters feared that Kalākaua had great strength in the legislature. They got the legislature to pass a motion requiring each member to sign his name on the back of his ballot. All votes were for Lunalilo. The people had won. Later, Queen Emma wrote in a letter that hundreds of Hawaiians were ready to tear to pieces any member who opposed Lunalilo.

Lunalilo's coronation was held at Kawaiahaʻo Church in a truly royal ceremony. The church was filled, and an even larger crowd stood outside. Lunalilo walked to the church, refusing to borrow a carriage.

In many ways Lunalilo brought strength to the throne, although he had certain weaknesses. At the Chiefs' Children's School, he was a good student, excelling in literature and music. However, he had no training in practical matters or in public administration. The new king was intelligent and witty, but generous to a fault. He had a good sense of humor, but sometimes had difficulty in reaching a decision. He suffered from alcoholism and was in poor health.

As soon as he became king, Lunalilo asked the legislature to change the constitution. The most important change he asked for was the removal of property qualifications for voters. Another thing he asked for was the separation of the legislature into two houses, the House of Nobles and the House of Representatives.

Prince Lunalilo, before becoming king in 1873. Hawaiʻi State Archives

coronation: a ceremony in which a king or queen is crowned and begins ruling

excelling: doing especially well

The Honolulu Chamber of Commerce asked the king to try again to secure a treaty allowing Hawaiian sugar to enter the United States tax-free. Island Curio

Economic Problems

When Lunalilo became king, there was an economic depression in Hawai'i. The whaling fleets were gone. Sugar exports had dropped because of the United States' tariff. The price of sugar was low, and labor costs were high. These unfavorable conditions in the sugar industry affected the entire nation.

The Honolulu Chamber of Commerce asked the king to try again to secure a treaty allowing Hawaiian sugar to enter the United States tax-free. The king discussed with his cabinet the idea of offering the United States Pearl Harbor in exchange for the tax-free admission of Hawaiian sugar. Hawaiians as well as some foreigners opposed the idea. When it became clear that the legislature would not approve giving territory to a foreign power, the offer was withdrawn.

Landing Hawaiian sugar in San Francisco tax-free was

so important for Hawai'i's economy that once more there was talk of annexation to the United States if a trade treaty could not be secured. However, most Hawaiians did not support annexation, and the United States had little interest in Hawai'i. High American tariffs caused sugar planters to consider a treaty with Australia and New Zealand. However, the entire question of a trade treaty was set aside for the rest of Lunalilo's short reign.

Hansen's Disease Laws Enforced

On the advice of the Board of Health, the laws for isolating Hansen's disease patients were strictly enforced. The people did not understand the seriousness of the disease or the importance of isolating patients. To them, being sent to the settlement on Moloka'i was the same as a death sentence.

In 1873, 560 people were sent to the Kalaupapa settlement, doubling its population. It was difficult for the small settlement to handle that number. Every effort was made to meet the emergency with the small amount of money the legislature had set aside. A pipeline was installed to bring fresh water to the patients. Father Damien, the leading figure in the story of the Kalaupapa settlement, arrived that same year. He died of the disease in 1889. Today, medical treatment controls Hansen's disease, so patients no longer need to be isolated.

In 1873, Father Damien moved to Kalaupapa to offer comfort and spiritual guidance to people dying of leprosy. He too died of the disease. Guava Graphics

A statue of Father Damien stands at the mauka entrance to the Hawai'i State Capitol in Honolulu. B. Bess

Father Damien was buried at the Kalaupapa Settlement on Moloka'i, but his remains were returned to his home in Belgium in the 1930s. Island Curio

The kingdom's sixty-man army was named the Household Troops. In 1873, the group mutinied against the officer in command and the drill master. As a result, the king disbanded the Household Troops. Hawai'i State Archives

Mutiny of the Household Troops

In September 1873 the kingdom's sixty-man army, called the Household Troops, mutinied. The men revolted against the officer in command and the drill master. Neither of these was Hawaiian. Any attempt to put down the mutiny by force might have led to civil war and violence toward most of the foreigners in the kingdom. After the king persuaded the mutineers to lay down their arms and go home, he disbanded the Household Troops.

disbanded: broke up

The Death of Lunalilo

While the mutiny was taking place, the king was quite ill. He had developed a lung infection that within a few months would lead to his death from tuberculosis. The king went to Kailua on the island of Hawai'i to try to win back his health. He refused to choose an heir, saying it was up to the people.

The talk of annexation and cession of Pearl Harbor encouraged anti-American feelings. These were encouraged by the writings of Walter Murray Gibson (see chapters 10 and 13). The anti-missionary attitude was further shown by Queen Emma, who was pro-British and favored the Church of England. In the legislative elections, almost all the men elected were Hawaiians who supported Kalākaua.

In January the king, whose health had grown worse, returned to Honolulu. He died on February 3, 1874. In his will he provided for building a home for old and poor Hawaiians. It is known today as Lunalilo Home.

Lunalilo asked to be buried next to his mother on the grounds of Kawaiahaʻo Church rather than at the Royal Mausoleum in Nuʻunau Valley.

cession: the giving up of control to someone else

Summing Up the Chapter

Since Kamehameha V had not named an heir to the throne, the legislature had to choose. William C. Lunalilo and David Kalākaua were the chief candidates. Lunalilo, who was the choice of the people, won all the votes. The new king tried to make the government more democratic. There was talk of giving Pearl Harbor to the United States in exchange for a treaty by which Hawaiian sugar would enter the United States tax-free. There was even talk of annexation, although it was not favored by Hawaiians. The Hansen's disease laws were strictly enforced. Father Damien began to work with the patients on Molokaʻi in 1873. The king disbanded the Household Troops after a short mutiny. Lunalilo would not name an heir to the throne, and his death from tuberculosis left the kingdom without a king once more.

Lunalilio asked to be buried next to his mother on the grounds of the Kawaiahaʻo Church rather than at the Royal Mausoleum in Nuʻuanu Valley.
B. Bess

13
The Reign of Kalākaua
(1874–1891)

David Kalākaua. Kawaiaha'o Church

Since Lunalilo did not name an heir, it was again necessary for the legislature to elect a king.

The day following Lunalilo's death, Colonel David Kalākaua announced his candidacy for the throne. Kalākaua had much support among the *ali'i* and the common people, particularly those from the Neighbor Islands. Most of the foreigners, including the Americans, were also for Kalākaua.

The next day Queen Emma, the widow of Kamehameha IV, said that she too was a candidate for the throne. Queen Emma had close ties to the British community. While on a trip abroad, she had become good friends with England's Queen Victoria. Queen Emma and her husband had helped establish the Anglican Church in Hawai'i. Naturally, the English in Hawai'i supported Queen Emma.

Many thought that Kalākaua's election would mean closer ties with America. Queen Emma's election would mean closer ties with Great Britain.

David Kalākaua and Queen Emma were both candidates for the throne following the death of Lunalilo. Many thought that Kalākaua's election would mean closer ties with America. Queen Emma's election would mean closer ties with Great Britain. Kawaiaha'o Church

The Election of Kalākaua as King

The legislature met in the courthouse on February 12, 1874, to elect a new king. Thirty-nine members voted for Kalākaua and six for Queen Emma.

A crowd made up mostly of Queen Emma's supporters had gathered outside. When a committee of the legislature tried to leave the courthouse, the mob tore their carriage to pieces. The committee members, barely escaping with their lives, sought safety in the courthouse as the mob forced its way into the building. The non-Hawaiian members of the legislature were not harmed by the mob. Hawaiian legislators who could not escape were savagely beaten. One of the legislators was thrown out of a window and another died of injuries a few days later.

In order to prevent further rioting and loss of life, Kalākaua, together with Minister of Foreign Affairs Charles R. Bishop, and O'ahu's Governor John O. Dominis, asked the American and British representatives to land marines from three warships anchored in the harbor. Sailors and marines restored order by evening. They remained onshore for a week, until the new government became firmly established.

Kalākaua had hoped for a grand coronation at Kawaiaha'o Church. Instead, because of the riot, he had a simple coronation

John O. Dominis. Guava Graphics

129

King Kalākaua, *left*, and Queen Kapi'olani, *third from left,* on the 'Iolani Palace grounds. Hawai'i State Archives

performed as quickly and quietly as possible. On February 13, 1874, at noon, Kalākaua took the oath of office. That same day, Queen Emma recognized him as king. She asked her supporters to do the same.

What sort of man was Kalākaua? He came from a line of high chiefs of the island of Hawai'i. His queen, Kapi'olani, came from the ruling family of Kaua'i. Kalākaua was well educated. He could speak English and Hawaiian fluently. He loved music and the arts. During his reign he tried to bring back ancient customs, including hula. Although Kalākaua was nicknamed the "merrie monarch," he took his royal duties seriously.

Kalākaua believed that the great chiefs had a hereditary right to rule and that the king should be the real ruler of the

fluently: smoothly and easily

hereditary: passed from one family member to another

country. Before becoming king he had gained much experience as an administrator and as a legislator. The Constitution of 1864 gave the king broad powers, and he used them to achieve his purposes. To strengthen his position, Kalākaua followed the old Hawaiian custom of touring the kingdom to meet as many people as possible. His trip gave the people renewed confidence. To them he was *ali'i nui* (a great chief).

Reciprocity

Kalākaua came to the throne during an economic depression in Hawai'i. To improve the economy, he decided to try again for a reciprocity treaty with the United States. Chief Justice E. H. Allen and H. A. P. Carter left for Washington in October 1874 to negotiate a treaty.

In support of the treaty, Kalākaua himself sailed for San Francisco in November as a guest of the United States. With him were his brother-in-law, Governor John O. Dominis of O'ahu, Governor John M. Kapena of Maui, and Henry A. Peirce, United States minister to Hawai'i. The guns of the forts of San Francisco boomed their welcome. The leaders of the city arranged entertainment suitable for a king. The United States government provided a special train to take the king from San Francisco to Washington, D.C.

Kalākaua was received by President Ulysses S. Grant and invited to appear before both houses of Congress. He made a great impression on Washington, both diplomatically and socially. He also visited New York and Boston. After three months, he returned to Honolulu.

In the meantime, negotiations for the treaty were taking place. Louisiana sugar interests and New Englanders trading in West Indian sugar opposed the treaty, but it was finally signed in January 1875. It went into effect the following year. Many people in both countries had fought against it. The Hawaiians who objected to the treaty thought that it made their country more dependent than ever on the United States. They thought it would cause Hawai'i to be taken over by the United States.

The treaty allowed many Hawaiian goods, particularly unrefined sugar and rice, to be admitted into the United States duty-free. In exchange, a number of American products would be admitted duty-free to Hawai'i. Hawai'i agreed not to make a similar treaty with any other nation. The treaty was to run for

A *pā'ū* rider at the Merrie Monarch Festival, an annual festival named in honor of King Kalākaua, affectionately referred to by the people of Hawai'i as the "merrie monarch" because of his love of music and dance. B. Bess

negotiate: to reach an agreement through discussion

at least seven years. When it was renewed in 1887, it gave the United States exclusive use of Pearl Harbor.

How Sugar Production Expanded

The reciprocity treaty gave Hawai'i a firm base for its growing sugar industry. In 1875, twenty-five million pounds of sugar were exported. Just fifteen years later exports had risen to ten times that amount. How was it possible to expand sugar production so rapidly?

As more money was made from the sale of sugar, more money could be spent to expand existing plantations and start new ones. Mainland capital flowed more rapidly into Hawai'i for investment in sugar plantations, irrigation projects, and sugar mills.

Most of the boom resulted from the hard work of men already in Hawai'i. One exception was Claus Spreckels. He had not favored the reciprocity treaty, because he had made a fortune from beet sugar in California. But after the treaty went into effect, he lost no time in coming to Hawai'i. He bought land on Maui for a large sugar plantation.

Sugar needs a great deal of water—both to grow the cane and to process it at the mill. One pound of sugar in the sugar bowl must have two thousand pounds of water to grow the cane from which the sugar is made. About half the sugar was grown on land that receives less than the average rainfall of seventy-five inches needed to grow sugarcane without irrigation. In order to have more land for sugar production, the growers developed large irrigation projects.

The first of the big irrigation projects was the seventeen-mile Hāmākua Ditch on Maui. It was built by S. T. Alexander and H. P. Baldwin to bring forty million gallons of water a day from the wet side of Haleakalā to their plantation on the dry plain of central Maui. As construction was nearing completion, the workers refused to lower themselves by rope, hand over hand, into the deep gorge of Māliko Gulch. H. P. Baldwin, who had lost one arm in an accident, slid down the rope himself, using his legs and his one arm. Ashamed, the workmen followed. Mr. Baldwin went into the gulch with his men every day until the job was completed.

Claus Spreckels followed the example of Alexander and Baldwin and built a ditch thirty miles long that delivered fifty

Californian Claus Spreckels was called the "sugar king" because of his success in the sugar production business.
Hawai'i State Archives

57. INTERIOR OF SUGAR MILL, HAWAIIAN ISLANDS.

New machines, mills, and the expansion of the sugar factoring system aided the growth of the sugar industry.
Island Curio

million gallons of water a day to his lands in central Maui. A third ditch was dug a few years later. The dry, dusty plain of central Maui began to yield rich crops of sugar. Other islands copied the Maui irrigation system.

The technology for sugar production also was improving. Samuel Burbank had invented a deep plow at Kōloa Plantation some years earlier. Fertilizer was used more effectively to aid the growth of sugarcane. A machine for separating sugar from molasses made it possible to make high-grade sugar at lower costs.

New sugar mills were built. The Honolulu Iron Works expanded its facilities to manufacture equipment for the plantations.

The expansion of the factoring system also aided the growth of the sugar industry. The factors were business agents for the plantations. They took care of the sale and shipping of the sugar crops. They bought supplies, insured crops, and financed many of the plantations. As the sugar industry expanded, the owners

The Bureau of Immigration was created to find workers in other countries for the plantations. Laborers received wages and living benefits for their work. Hawai'i State Archives

of poorly managed plantations had to turn over stock to the factors. In some cases these factors took over the management and even the ownership to keep the plantations producing sugar.

In 1882 the planters and their agents formed an organization to share information about problems they all faced. It came to be known as the Planter's Labor and Supply Company.

One problem was the supply of cheap labor. A Bureau of Immigration was created to find workers in other countries. Almost all imported laborers got free food, shelter, and medical care, as well as wages. At the end of the contract period, laborers were given free passage back to their native lands if they did not want to stay in Hawai'i. Many plantation workers returned to their native countries. Some went to the United States mainland, where they thought there was greater opportunity. Finding labor for the plantations was a constant problem.

Water Transportation

Before the reciprocity treaty, most interisland traffic was carried on by sailing vessels. In 1877 Samuel G. Wilder organized the Wilder Steamship Company and put several steamers into service. In 1905 that company joined with another to form the Inter-Island Steam Navigation Company. It became the parent of the present Hawaiian Airlines.

In 1867, the postmaster general of the United States made a contract for monthly mail service between Honolulu and the West Coast with the California, Oregon and Mexico Steamship Company. For many years after 1875 the Pacific Mail Steamship Company maintained a service between San Francisco and Australia, stopping at Honolulu. Claus Spreckels' son organized the Oceanic Steamship Company in 1882. It offered regular service between San Francisco and Honolulu, and later to Australia and New Zealand. In 1882 Captain William Matson began a shipping line that later controlled water traffic between

Postage stamps issued during the Monarchy period. Island Curio

The Oʻahu Railway and Land Company was started by Benjamin F. Dillingham on November 16, 1889. The company's terminal building is on the left. Hawaiʻi State Archives

Oʻahu Railway and Land Co. train.
Hawaii State Archives

Hawaiʻi and the mainland. Matson added one steamship after another, as his line expanded to carry cargo to and from the Islands.

Railroad and Land Transportation

The story of railroading on Oʻahu centers chiefly on one man, Benjamin F. Dillingham. He was a sailor who stopped in Hawaiʻi in 1865. He was thrown from a horse and broke his leg. His ship sailed on. After he recovered he decided to stay in Hawaiʻi. With the help of Alfred Castle he went into business. He began to buy farmlands. Realizing that the development of the land depended on cheap and efficient transportation, Dillingham and others, including James Campbell, started the Oʻahu Railway and Land Company. Soon Dillingham expanded the railroad to most of the island. He encouraged the establishment of sugar plantations on the new land opened by the railroad. He filled in swamps and built wharves and warehouses for shipping sugar and handling general cargo.

With the growth of the sugar and rice industries, railroads alone did not provide enough land transportation. The government began to spend large sums of money building roads and bridges. By 1888 Honolulu had its first mule-drawn streetcar. Soon this streetcar route was extended to Waikīkī, considered to be quite far from downtown Honolulu.

Kalākaua's Cabinets

Kalākaua made full use of the king's right to appoint and dismiss cabinet members. The lines were sharply drawn between the king's party and the missionary party. Both sides used newspapers to get support for their views.

The first cabinet Kalākaua appointed was generally acceptable to all sides. But in 1876 Kalākaua dismissed this cabinet and appointed a new one. The missionary party objected. They believed Hawai'i should be a constitutional monarchy, like England. The king should be respected, but should have little real power over the government. They believed that the legislature should control the cabinet ministers.

In 1878 Claus Spreckels, a wealthy Californian, bought land on Maui for a sugar plantation. Spreckels needed water for irrigation. He applied to the cabinet for water rights and was turned down. By means of a loan he persuaded Kalākaua to dismiss the cabinet and appoint a new cabinet. The new cabinet gave Spreckels the water rights.

A few years later, Spreckels offered to lend the kingdom $1,000,000 in exchange for the right to open a bank. Spreckels finally agreed to pay for the minting of $1,000,000 in coins, with the head of Kalākaua on them, in exchange for government bonds. It is claimed that Spreckels made an additional $150,000 in minting the coins.

In 1883, Claus Spreckels agreed to pay for the minting of $1,000,000 in coins. The coins were decorated with Kalākaua's profile and the Hawaiian coat of arms. Hawai'i State Archives

A one-hundred-dollar certificate of deposit, issued in 1879 or 1880. These certificates were backed by gold or silver. Hawai'i State Archives

scandal: a shameful event that is made public

More trouble arose over Celso Caesar Moreno, an Italian who had been authorized by the U. S. government to lay a telegraph cable between America and Asia. When a member of the cabinet was accused of being involved in a scandal, Kalākaua dismissed the cabinet and appointed a new one with Moreno as minister of foreign affairs.

Hawaiians appeared to support Moreno. The non-Hawaiians in the kingdom were angry at his appointment. Five days later, Moreno resigned. Kalākaua then placed him in charge of three Anglo-Hawaiian boys who were to be educated abroad.

In the meantime the missionary party insisted on an all-foreign cabinet of their choosing. The king agreed, but he appointed three Hawaiians to the privy council, along with Walter Murray Gibson, a supporter of the king and the Hawaiian people.

The attempt to limit the king's power through a constitutional monarchy was the basis of the political struggle during Kalākaua's reign. This struggle finally resulted in the Constitution of 1887, which stripped the king of much of his political power.

The Trip around the World

By promoting the growth and sale of sugar, the reciprocity treaty brought a greater demand than ever for laborers. In 1881, Kalākaua decided to make a trip around the world. He would meet other rulers and perhaps find more laborers for Hawai'i. He may also have had a political motive for the trip. By learning the ways of other rulers he hoped to better protect his own people.

Kauikeaouli Gate, located in front of the 'Iolani Palace, was decorated in honor of King Kalākaua's return home from his trip around the world in 1881.
Hawai'i State Archives

He prepared quickly for the trip. In 1877 Prince Leleiōhōkū, the king's brother and heir, had died, and Kalākaua named his sister, Princess Lili'uokalani, heiress to the throne. She became regent while he was away.

He sailed first to San Francisco, where he received a royal welcome. In Japan, the king was invited to be the guest of the emperor. Kalākaua was the first king of a Western nation to visit Japan and was treated with as much honor as the mightiest ruler on earth. He was received with equal respect by the rulers of other countries he visited.

Siam: a Southeast Asian country known today as Thailand

Burma: a Southeast Asian country known today as Myanmar

From Japan he traveled to China, Siam, Burma, India, and Egypt. In Italy he had an audience with the Pope. He also visited

The coronation of Kalākaua and Kapiʻolani took place on February 12, 1883. At the ceremony, Kalākaua placed his own crown on his head. Hawaiʻi State Archives

Belgium, Germany, Austria, France, Spain, and Portugal. In England he rode to Buckingham Palace in Queen Victoria's own coach. While in Europe, he ordered furnishings for ʻIolani Palace. He also ordered two jeweled crowns for the coronation he had planned on his return to Hawaiʻi.

The Coronation

On February 12, 1883, the new palace, homes, public buildings, and even foreign battleships in the harbor were decorated for the coronation. The ceremony included ancient Hawaiian ritual, along with customs Kalākaua had noted in European courts. It began with a recitation of the king's genealogy. Then other symbols of royalty were presented to the king, including the golden feather cloak of Kamehameha and the crowns. The king placed his crown on his own head and then placed one upon the queen's head.

While Kalākaua was in Europe, he ordered two crowns from England: one for himself, *top*, and the other for Queen Kapiʻolani, *bottom*.
Hawaiʻi State Archives

recitation: saying something out loud, from memory, for an audience

139

That evening, a ball was held, with singing and hula. Those who opposed the king were upset by the cost of the coronation. They were even more disturbed by the return of the hula, which they considered immoral.

Electricity and Telephones

King Kalākaua had a surprise for his guests at his inaugural ball. The throne room was lit with electric lights. This was the first use of electricity in the kingdom. It was not until 1891, when the Hawaiian Electric Company was started, that others could have electricity.

Charles Dickey came to Honolulu in 1878 to start the Hawaiian Bell Telephone Company. Less than two years after Alexander G. Bell obtained his patent on the telephone, Dickey had installed a telephone line between his home and the store he managed. King Kalākaua had a line strung between ʻIolani Palace and the royal boathouse.

Soon a second telephone company, the Mutual Telephone Company, was started. For a while there was a telephone war in Honolulu. Mutual finally bought out Hawaiian Bell and other companies on the Neighbor Islands.

Cultural Life of the Kingdom

Kalākaua wanted to revive and record ancient Hawaiian traditions. He formed a group, Ka Hale Nauā (The Temple of Wisdom), for research into the origins of mankind.

Kalākaua tried to preserve old chants, which, like the hula, had been forbidden by the missionaries. He assembled a group of the *kāhuna kuahau*, and each brought his ball of knotted *olonā* cord. At this gathering the ancient Hawaiian chant of creation, the *Kumulipo*, was recorded and preserved. Later, monthly meetings of the "Ball of Twine" society were held at the palace. The missionary group was angered by this attempt to restore the *kāhuna*. What made matters worse was the king's revival of the hula.

Kalākaua loved music. At the beginning of his reign, he and his sister and brother each had a musical group. They often composed original music, which they sang. Kalākaua wrote the words for the kingdom's national anthem, *"Hawaiʻi Ponoʻi."* It was set to music by Captain Henry Berger, who had been brought to Hawaiʻi to organize the Royal Hawaiian Band.

kāhuna kuahau: historians

On King Kalākaua's fiftieth birthday, he held a jubilee celebration at 'Iolani Palace. Graphic Works

Robert Louis Stevenson in Hawai'i

One of the important visitors to Hawai'i during Kalākaua's reign was the English writer Robert Louis Stevenson. He came to Hawai'i after spending six months in the South Sea Islands, where he came to love the Polynesian people and their way of life. He became a close friend of Kalākaua's.

At a *lū'au* in honor of the Stevensons, the king and Princess Lili'uokalani were special guests. The menu included baked dog, chicken, pig, *poi*, raw fish, cooked fish, crabs, *limu*, and

poi: food made from pounded and watered taro; it is sometimes made from breadfruit or sweet potato.

limu: seaweed

141

A *lūʻau* was held in honor of the Stevensons. At the head of the table Princess Liliʻuokalani is seated between Robert Louis Stevenson and Kalākaua. Hawaiʻi State Archives

kukui: tree whose oily nuts were used for lamps

roasted *kukui* nuts. Mrs. Stevenson gave the king a rare pearl. The closing lines of a poem Mr. Stevenson wrote for the occasion read

> To golden hands the golden pearl I bring:
> The ocean jewel to the island king.

Stevenson lived in Waikīkī, next door to ʻĀinahau, the home of Princess Kaʻiulani. He and Kaʻiulani became friends. They spent pleasant hours under the banyan tree at ʻĀinahau, where he told her many fascinating tales.

When Stevenson learned that Kaʻiulani was unhappy at leaving the Islands to study in England, he wrote a poem to comfort her. The first verse of "To Kaiulani" reads

Forth from her land to mine she goes,
The island maiden, the island rose,
Light of heart and bright of face,
The daughter of a double race.
Her islands here, in Southern sun,
Shall mourn their Kaiulani gone,
And I, in her dear banyan shade
Look vainly for my little maid.

Having heard about the work of Father Damien among the patients at Kalaupapa, Stevenson was eager to visit the settlement. Before he could get there, Damien had died of the disease. Stevenson went to the settlement anyway to see it for himself. When a letter criticizing Father Damien was published

English writer Robert Louis Stevenson and King Kalākaua became close friends during Stevenson's visit to Hawai'i. Hawai'i State Archives

Princess Ka'iulani was well-loved by the people of Hawai'i and was affectionately referred to as "the people's princess." Graphic Works

143

in an Australian newspaper, Stevenson wrote an angry reply to the writer. He turned over all money received for the publication of material he had written in defense of Father Damien to the fund for the patients.

Education

During this period an increasing number of American education practices were adopted in Hawai'i. Although English had been the language of business and government since 1850, most children enrolled in the common schools were taught in the Hawaiian language. The rest of the students attended government English schools or private schools. The number of schools in which English was taught rose steadily.

Control and administration of the schools also changed during this period. An appointed school board hired a superintendent and made policy. The superintendents had been trained in America, and the policies they recommended followed American patterns. Local school committees hired teachers.

Toward the end of the monarchy, American textbooks were adopted, bought by the board, and sold to the students at cost. School buildings and equipment were improved.

Teachers had to take an examination for certification. Teacher training improved. English classes for adults were started.

By the end of the monarchy, only 10,700 children attended public schools. However, the curriculum for these children had been improved.

Walter Murray Gibson

Kalākaua's strongest supporter and the greatest enemy of the missionary party was probably Walter Murray Gibson. He came to Hawai'i as a Mormon missionary and started a Mormon settlement on Lāna'i. He later moved to Honolulu. There he established an English-Hawaiian newspaper in 1873 to fight annexation. Through his newspaper he supported the election of Kalākaua. After Kalākaua was elected, Gibson stopped publishing his paper and returned to Lāna'i.

Gibson was elected to the legislature in 1878 and became a leading figure in the king's party. In the legislature he supported bills to improve the health of Hawaiians, to build 'Iolani Palace, and to create a statue of Kamehameha. Gibson

'Iolani Palace was built in 1882. Graphic Works

supported the building of 'Iolani Palace from his personal funds. He even went into debt for the project. In 1882 Gibson was appointed head of the cabinet and remained in office until 1887.

Although Gibson may not have had more than an eighth-grade education, he spoke several foreign languages. Even his enemies considered him intelligent and well mannered. He rarely became upset, even when mistreated by his enemies. He was completely loyal to the Hawaiian people and their king. Gibson told Hawaiians not to hate foreigners but to remember the good things they had brought. He also encouraged Hawaiians to be hopeful about the future.

Not everyone approved of Gibson, however. Some of the king's opponents plotted unsuccessfully to assassinate Gibson and to cause trouble during the coronation. Opponents blamed

Gibson for spending too much on the coronation and on the Board of Genealogy.

Attempts at Empire Building

During this period, the United States, Britain, France, and Germany were taking control of islands in the Pacific. Gibson encouraged Kalākaua's dream of forming a Polynesian confederation. The king hoped that the islands, by joining together, could keep their independence. The king of Samoa agreed to join politically with Hawai'i, but the German government threatened to use force if Hawai'i or the Americans made trouble for the Germans in Samoa. In a show of military strength, Kalākaua refitted an old ship. But the boat was too small and its crew too undisciplined to have much effect. The king's dream ended in failure.

The Bayonet Constitution of 1887

During Kalākaua's reign, government spending and public debt had risen sharply. The missionary party thought the government spent too much money. The king's party thought they should be able to enjoy some of the wealth resulting from the reciprocity treaty.

Some Hawaiians wanted to drive the *haole* from the land and restore the ancient Hawaiian culture. In January 1887, a group of foreigners formed a secret political group called the Hawaiian League. Most of its members wanted a constitutional monarchy. Some of its members wanted the overthrow of the monarchy and annexation to the United States.

In June the Hawaiian League held a mass meeting. Outside was a military unit, the Hawaiian Rifles. They supposedly served the Hawaiian government, but were secretly controlled by the League.

The king gave in to the League's demands. Even before the mass meeting, he removed Gibson from office. Gibson was arrested by the commander of the Hawaiian Rifles. He wanted to hang Gibson. The League refused to go along with him. Gibson left Hawai'i and died six months later in San Francisco.

The king also agreed to a new cabinet selected by the Committee of Thirteen (made up of members of the Hawaiian League). It included W. L. Green, Godfrey Brown, Lorrin A. Thurston, and Clarence W. Ashford.

confederation: a group of countries joined together for a common purpose

146

A military unit called the Hawaiian Rifles supposedly served the Hawaiian government, but was secretly controlled by the Hawaiian League. Hawai'i State Archives

Five days after the new cabinet was formed, the members presented the king with a new constitution. This Bayonet Constitution of 1887 was a revision of Kamehameha V's Constitution of 1864. After several hours of argument, Kalākaua signed this document. He had no choice, since the League controlled the military forces.

The constitution took away most of the king's power. He was allowed to do nothing without the approval of the cabinet. He could still appoint the cabinet, but he could not dismiss it without the approval of the legislature. He could not organize any military or naval forces without approval from the legislature.

The new constitution also made important changes in the

legislature. The nobles were to be elected instead of appointed by the king. Because of the financial requirements for both candidates and voters, mostly non-Hawaiians would elect the nobles. Any man over twenty who could read and write English, Hawaiian, or a European language and who had lived in Hawai'i for one year could vote if he took an oath to uphold the constitution and paid his taxes. This allowed foreigners to vote for representatives without becoming citizens of Hawai'i.

Wilcox's Revolt

The cabinet decided to bring home the Hawaiian youths who had been educated abroad at government expense. Among these was Robert Wilcox. He was a graduate in engineering and military science of the Royal Military Academy of Turin, Italy. He dreamed of leading Hawai'i to greatness.

Soon after his return, Wilcox began meeting with others who wanted to restore power to Hawaiians and their king. Some say he only wanted to help Kalākaua and drive the foreigners from political power. Others say he also wanted to replace Kalākaua with the king's sister and heir, Lili'uokalani. At dawn on July 30, 1889, Wilcox led a group of 150 men into the palace grounds and took control.

Wilcox invited the king to come to the palace to sign a new constitution. Kalākaua refused to come. The cabinet acted quickly to put down the revolt. They called out the Honolulu Rifles and armed the government officials with rifles. From buildings surrounding the palace, they fired upon Wilcox's men. The next morning Wilcox surrendered. Seven men had been killed and twelve wounded. Wilcox was charged with conspiracy and tried before an all-Hawaiian jury. As expected, he was found not guilty.

Events Favoring the King

Although military action did not help the king, he won the support of many people who were able to help him. Chinese merchants hired large numbers of Hawaiians at a high enough salary to enable them to vote. A group calling itself the Political Economy Party, whose members were native Hawaiians, worked to restore the Constitution of 1864. The king's party grew stronger as the elections for the legislature of 1889 approached.

Robert William Wilcox led a revolt to change the leadership in the Hawaiian kingdom. Guava Graphics

conspiracy: an agreement between two or more people to do something criminal or illegal

On January 20, 1891, King Kalākaua died in San Francisco. His body was returned to Hawai'i aboard the USS *Charleston*. Hawai'i State Archives

The Death of the King

The king was ill when, in 1890, he left for San Francisco aboard the cruiser *Charleston*. As before, the king was given a warm welcome, but his health became worse. He died there on January 20, 1891. His body was returned to Hawai'i aboard the *Charleston*.

The *Charleston* was sighted off Diamond Head at dawn. As the ship came closer, the lookout saw the flag at half-mast. The news spread rapidly. Soon all flags were flying at half-mast. The arches and buildings decorated to celebrate the king's homecoming were quickly draped in black. Kalākaua was buried with great ceremony.

Before the king was buried, the cabinet insisted Lili'uokalani take the oath of office as queen. This ended the period of elected kings.

Queen Kapiʻolani presented a flag and calabash to the officers of the USS *Charleston* in gratitude for the high honor and consideration the U.S. showed in the events surrounding King Kalākaua's death.
Hawaiʻi State Archives

Summing Up the Chapter

The election of Kalākaua rather than Queen Emma to the throne meant that American influence would be stronger than English influence in Hawaiʻi. Although he was known as the "merrie monarch," Kalākaua was a strong ruler who tried to build up his nation. He visited the United States to promote a trade treaty between the two countries. Under the new treaty, unrefined sugar and rice, as well as some other Hawaiian goods, could enter the United States tax-free.

Because of a favorable reciprocity treaty with the United States, Hawaiian planters wanted to produce as much sugar as possible. To increase the amount of land that could be used for sugar, water was brought in through long irrigation ditches. Methods of producing sugar were improved. Workers were brought from other countries under a contract system.

Interisland and transpacific steamship service was started. By the end of Kalākaua's reign, railroads operated on three of the islands. Electricity and telephones came to the Islands before the end of the century.

Kalākaua tried to keep alive early Hawaiian culture. He also encouraged the development of music. Robert Louis Stevenson visited the Islands at that time and was a friend of Kalākaua's and of the royal family's. During this period, American patterns of school administration and teaching methods were applied to the Hawaiian public school system.

A long and bitter struggle went on between Kalākaua and the constitutional reformers. Probably the strongest supporter of the king was Walter Murray Gibson, who was head of the cabinet from 1882 to 1887.

Kalākaua dreamed of heading a great Polynesian confederation, but he was not able to win the support of more powerful nations. Kalākaua's enemies accused him of spending too much money. A Hawaiian League was formed that wanted to overthrow the monarchy and join the Islands to the United States. The king dismissed Gibson from office and was forced to agree to a new constitution, which took away much of his political power. This so-called Bayonet Constitution of 1887 was a revision of Kamehameha's Constitution of 1864.

Robert Wilcox, a Hawaiian youth who had studied abroad at government expense, tried without success to use force to restore the land to the Hawaiians and their king. Two years later a compromise cabinet was formed. However, the struggle had been too much for Kalākaua. He died in San Francisco in 1891 and his body was returned to Hawai'i. His sister, Lili'uokalani, who had been acting as regent, became queen.

14
Queen Liliʻuokalani, the Overthrow of the Monarchy, and Annexation (1887–1901)

Queen Liliʻuokalani came to the throne in 1891. Her reign ended abruptly with the overthrow of the monarchy by the United States in 1893. In 1895 she was imprisoned for her supposed connection to a conspiracy to regain control of the kingdom. After she was released, she led a modest life until her death on November 11, 1917.
Graphic Works

When the news of the king's death reached Hawai'i, the cabinet wanted Lili'uokalani to be named queen immediately. They also insisted that she take the oath of office, which included a promise to uphold and defend the Constitution of 1887.

Background of a Queen

The queen was born on September 2, 1838. She was named Liliu Kamaka'eha. She was given her Christian name, Lydia, at her baptism. Her brother, King Kalākaua, asked her to take the name Lili'uokalani when she agreed to be his heir.

At the age of four she was enrolled in the Royal School. There she was educated along with four other rulers of Hawai'i.

In 1862, she married John Owen Dominis, who would later be governor of O'ahu. They lived with his parents at Washington Place, today the home of Hawai'i's governor. When Dominis died, shortly after Lili'uokalani came to the throne, the queen lost a valued adviser.

She spent much of her life at the royal court. During

Queen Kapi'olani, seated, and Princess Lili'uokalani in London, England.
Hawai'i State Archives

Queen Kapi'olani and Princess Lili'uokalani, center, with their British hosts, in London to attend the Diamond Jubilee of Queen Victoria. Hawai'i State Archives

153

The National Reform Party supported Lili'uokalani. Guava Graphics

The Reverend Lorrin A. Thurston headed the Reform Party. Formerly, he was principal of the Lahainaluna Seminary and a judge of cases involving foreigners. Guava Graphics

Kalākaua's two trips abroad, she acted as regent. In 1887 she went with Queen Kapi'olani, her sister-in-law, to the Diamond Jubilee of Queen Victoria. While on this trip, she learned of the constitution that Kalākaua had been forced to sign. She was so upset that she canceled a tour of the rest of Europe and returned to Hawai'i at once. There she found the Hawaiian people fearful of losing their independence.

Trouble Begins

Queen Lili'uokalani came to the throne in 1891, during a difficult time for the sugar industry and for Hawai'i's economy. The United States had changed its tariff policy. The McKinley Tariff allowed sugar from all countries to enter the United States duty-free. Sugar growers in the United States got price supports. Hawai'i no longer had the advantages it had under the reciprocity treaty. Many businessmen thought annexation to the United States would solve the problem.

The struggle for political power, which began under Kalākaua, broke out again in 1892. Men from three political parties made up the legislature. The National Reform Party supported the queen. The Reform Party, headed by Lorrin A. Thurston, did not want the queen's power increased. The Liberal Party was headed by a group, including Robert W. Wilcox, who had been arrested for plotting treason.

The major issues of the 1892 legislature were the cabinet and the constitution. These issues led directly to the overthrow of the monarchy.

When Lili'uokalani became queen, she appointed cabinet members from the National Reform Party, which supported her views. This cabinet was voted out of office as soon as the legislature met. The queen then appointed two more cabinets from among her followers. These also were voted out of office. After this, to avoid delay in carrying on state business, she named a cabinet made up of Reform Party members. The Liberal Party leaders were unhappy because they had not been named to the cabinet. Some of them joined with the National Reform Party to overthrow the Reform Party ministry, then in office. The queen again appointed members of her party, the National Reform Party, to the cabinet two days before the legislature ended.

While in session, the legislature passed lottery and opium bills. They expected the lottery to provide additional income.

They thought that if they made importing opium legal, its sale would be easier to control.

A new constitution had been discussed since 1887, when the Bayonet Constitution was adopted. In 1890 and 1892, Kalākaua and Liliʻuokalani had backed proposals to change or rewrite the constitution. Both times these measures were voted down. The queen's opponents voted down a bill to hold a constitutional convention to end property qualifications for voting.

Overthrow of the Monarchy

The defeat of the voting bill raised a cry of protest across the kingdom. Petitions bearing thousands of signatures poured into ʻIolani Palace. They asked the queen to issue a new constitution, just as Kamehameha V had.

The queen proposed to her ministers a constitution that would end property qualifications for voting and deny the right to vote to foreigners who were not Hawaiian citizens. It would also allow the queen to appoint nobles. Two of the ministers agreed to sign the new constitution. The rest feared trouble from the queen's opponents. After two hours of discussion the queen gave in to her ministers, but her opponents had already decided to overthrow her.

Annexation Club ledger signed by citizens of Honolulu.
Hawaiʻi State Archives

The Committee of Public Safety. Chairman Henry E. Cooper is pictured in the center. Hawai'i State Archives

On the Saturday before, the Annexation Club, which had been formed in the spring of 1892, had formed a Committee of Public Safety. They created a secret plan to do away with the monarchy, set up a provisional government, and apply to the United States for annexation.

When the meeting of the annexationists became known, the Hawaiians called a mass meeting for the same hour in Palace Square for all those who were against annexation. The chairman, Antone Rosa, presented a resolution pledging loyalty to the queen and promising to support her plan to seek constitutional changes only by legal means.

But the plans of the annexationists were already in motion. The Committee of Public Safety had asked U.S. Minister John L. Stevens to land troops. At five o'clock on Monday, January 16, 1893, a force of 162 heavily armed sailors and marines came ashore from the USS *Boston*. They marched down King Street to Arion Hall (across from 'Iolani Palace), where they spent the night.

Governor A. S. Cleghorn, father of Princess Ka'iulani, the

provisional: for the time being, temporary

156

heir to the throne, protested to Stevens. He said that the landing of troops violated international law and that he would enter a formal protest to the American government.

In the meantime, annexationist Sanford B. Dole at first proposed that Queen Lili'uokalani give up the throne in favor of Princess Ka'iulani. Later, Dole agreed to head the new government.

The actual overthrow of the monarchy, on January 17, 1893, was fairly orderly, except for a single unplanned event that helped the annexationists. The office where the final plans for the provisional government were made was being watched by a half-dozen policemen. They had orders to arrest members

A. S. Cleghorn was the governor of Hawai'i and the father of Princess Kai'ulani. Hawai'i State Archives

Lili'uokalani's staff on the 'Iolani Palace lānai. Hawai'i State Archives

While the provisional government was being put in place, the country was ruled by martial law. Hawai'i State Archives

of the Committee of Public Safety who headed toward the palace. When the policemen who had been on guard went to investigate a shooting, the committee members were free to go take over the government building.

With practically no audience, except the government clerks, Henry A. Cooper read the document the committee had written. It ended the monarchy and set up a provisional government until terms of union with the United States could be agreed upon. As the reading neared its end, a letter announcing the overthrow of the monarchy was sent to United States minister Stevens. He replied with a letter recognizing the provisional government.

The pistol shot that had enabled the committee to carry out its plan had been fired by the driver of a wagonload of ammunition being transported to the annexationists. The shot hit the policeman who had tried to stop the wagon. The wounded policeman was carried to the hospital by some of his fellow policemen who should have been watching the office.

The provisional government was in control. The queen, wishing to avoid bloodshed, had refused to allow military action against the annexationists. She believed that the American government would refuse to support these actions, just as England had done in the case of Lord Paulet.

The Provisional Government

The provisional government immediately ordered the people to turn in all weapons. The country was under the rule of martial law. Two weeks after the revolution the American flag was raised over the government building. Queen Liliʻuokalani withdrew to Washington Place.

People had to take an oath of allegiance to the new government. Some people took the oath to protect their jobs with the government. Rather than take the oath, the men of the Royal Hawaiian Band resigned. Many patriotic songs were written and sung. The most famous of these was *Mele ʻAi Pōhaku* ("Stone-Eating Song"). The words said that Hawaiians would eat stones rather than sign the oath to the provisional government and be disloyal to their queen.

The new administration sent a commission, headed by

Rather than take an oath of allegiance to the new government, members of the Royal Hawaiian Band resigned and the group was disbanded. Hawaiʻi State Archives

159

Princess Kaʻiulani and Theo. Davies.
Hawaiʻi State Archives

paramount: of highest rank or power

James Blount was appointed by President Cleveland to investigate the overthrow of the monarchy.
Hawaiʻi State Archives

amnesty: pardon; forgiveness, with no threat of punishment

Lorrin A. Thurston, to Washington to make a treaty of annexation with the United States. The queen also sent a commission. The queen's representatives were not allowed to board the planter-owned ship taking the provisional government's representatives to the United States. The delay gave the provisional government the advantage, since its representatives arrived in Washington first.

The timing was important. President Benjamin Harrison had ordered an annexation treaty drawn up. Some senators opposed it, and it had not been passed by the end of Harrison's term of office. When President Grover Cleveland came into office, he withdrew the treaty from the Senate. He may have been influenced by Princess Kaʻiulani, who came to Washington with her guardians, Mr. and Mrs. Theophilus Davies, to plead for the monarchy. There was much debate in the U.S. press about the revolution in Hawaiʻi and annexation.

President Cleveland appointed James Blount, a former chairman of the House Foreign Affairs Committee, to go to Hawaiʻi to investigate the overthrow. Since Blount's commission gave him power over all American officials and naval officers in Hawaiʻi, he was nicknamed "Paramount Blount." Blount tried to be fair to both sides.

Shortly after he arrived, Blount ordered that American flags be taken down and American troops be returned to their ship.

In his report, Blount charged that the revolution was the result of a conspiracy between Minister Stevens and the revolutionary leaders. He said that in a vote of all the citizens of the Islands, annexation to the United States would be defeated. On the basis of Blount's report, President Cleveland decided that the United States ought to undo the wrong done to Hawaiʻi and restore Queen Liliʻuokalani to her throne.

In the United States, the agents of the provisional government worked hard to stir up American support for annexation. The Republican Party was for annexation and the Democrats were against it.

President Cleveland sent Albert S. Willis to tell the queen that President Cleveland would restore her to the throne if she would forgive those who had overthrown her government. Just before Christmas the queen sent Willis a note stating that she would grant amnesty to all. She promised to work in peace and friendship for the good of the country.

Willis met with President Dole and the cabinet and read them the queen's message. He asked them to give the power back to the queen. President Dole sent Willis a long letter refusing to restore the monarchy. He said that the United States had no right to interfere in the internal affairs of Hawai'i. President Cleveland realized that the monarchy could not be restored without military force. He had to let the matter drop.

The leaders of the provisional government realized that President Cleveland would never allow annexation. They would have to wait until a different president was elected. In the meantime, they made plans for a more permanent form of government. On March 15, 1894, the Hawaiian legislature called for a constitutional convention to establish a republic.

The Organization of the Republic

From the start, the constitutional convention was controlled by the supporters of the revolution. The original draft of the proposed constitution was mostly the work of President Sanford Dole and Lorrin Thurston. It went into effect on July 4, 1894.

The constitution named Dole as president. The president's term of office was six years, and he could not succeed himself. The legislature would elect the president after Dole's term was over. The men who had headed the four departments under the

Sanford B. Dole, left, and Lorrin Andrews Thurston, right, drafted a constitution for the new Republic. Hawai'i State Archives

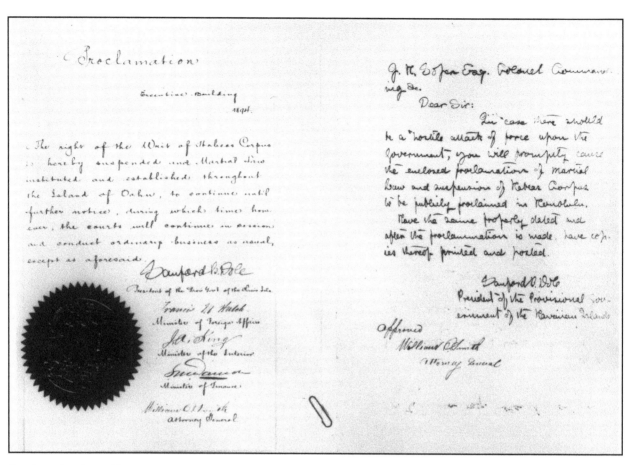

Proclamation issued by President Dole that established U. S. military control throughout the island of O'ahu.
Hawai'i State Archives

provisional government were reappointed by Dole to serve in the cabinet under the republic.

The legislature consisted of two houses—the Senate and the House of Representatives. Each house consisted of fifteen members. Membership in either branch of the legislature was open only to men of property. A certain degree of wealth was also required in order to vote for candidates for both houses of the legislature. Voters as well as members of the legislature had to take an oath to support the republic and promise not to try to bring back the monarchy. They also had to be able to speak, read, and write either Hawaiian or English. Parts of the constitution were designed to keep Asians and other newly arrived immigrants from becoming citizens.

It was a republic more in name than in actual fact since so few people could take part in the government.

In vain Queen Lili'uokalani protested the establishment of

the republic to both the United States and Great Britain. The new government was soon recognized by all countries with which it had diplomatic relations. On July 14, 1894, President Dole took the oath of office. The band played *"Hawai'i Pono'i,"* a new 36-foot flag was raised at the executive building, and the cannons boomed a national salute.

Counterrevolution

During the summer and fall of 1894 the supporters of the queen, led by men such as Samuel Nowlein, Robert Wilcox, Lot Kamehameha Lane, Charles T. Gulick, and William G. Rickard, plotted to overthrow the republic. Weapons were ordered and shipped from San Francisco.

Arms and ammunition were buried in the sands at the foot of Diamond Head. Rumors had put the government on guard. The revolt was completely put down within two weeks.

Although Queen Lili'uokalani knew of the plot, she did not actively take part in it. Nevertheless, she and her two nephews, Princes David Kawānanakoa and Jonah Kūhiō Kalaniana'ole, along with two hundred others, were arrested.

The prisoners were tried by a military court. In thirty-five days, 190 cases were tried and nearly all were found guilty.

Prince David Kawānanakoa with Queen Kapi'olani. Hawai'i State Archives

Following the attempted overthrow of the Republic, Queen Lili'uokalani was arrested and forced to spend eight months imprisoned in a room in 'Iolani Palace. Hawai'i State Archives

Prince Jonah Kūhiō Kalaniana'ole.
Hawai'i State Archives

163

The Executive Building ('Iolani Palace) was guarded by military officers shortly after Lili'uokalani's imprisonment. Hawai'i State Archives

Some were sentenced to death. The queen's sentence was five years imprisonment at hard labor and a fine of five thousand dollars. However, President Dole, the United States, and public opinion in Hawai'i were against the harsh sentences. The death sentences were changed to imprisonment.

Lili'uokalani spent eight months imprisoned in a room in 'Iolani Palace. During that time, she wrote down the words and music to *"Aloha 'Oe,"* a song she had composed years earlier.

By the end of 1895, under pressure from home and abroad, the republic released all remaining prisoners on parole. The government's victory over the revolutionists and its lenient treatment of them put the Republic of Hawai'i in a strong position at home and abroad.

lenient: not harsh or strict

Life under the Republic

Business in Hawai'i was given a boost by the passage of the Wilson-Gorman Act by the United States in 1894. American sugar producers no longer got a price support payment of two cents a pound, and foreign sugar imported into the United States was taxed. The Hawaiian sugar industry once

'Iolani Palace. Hawai'i State Archives

more profited from the special treatment it was given by the reciprocity treaty.

Under the republic, industry doubled or tripled. Many great fortunes were made. The planters built fine houses equal to mansions in New York or Chicago. They had baths, electric lights, and telephones.

Some Hawaiians felt the republic was a police state. Many large gatherings were broken up and people arrested on suspicion of treason. At one point, large gatherings were not allowed. The hula was forbidden and Sunday concerts were stopped. Finally, when Sunday concerts were allowed again, only European classical music could be played.

With the growth of the plantations, more laborers were needed. In the 1880s the government imported contract laborers from Japan to balance the great number of Chinese workers. In a few years, the Japanese made up about one-fourth of the population. Some people feared that Hawai'i might become a Japanese colony. Many things were tried to reduce the number of Japanese immigrants and increase the number of Chinese.

The planters tried to bring in more Caucasian workers, but this proved to be too expensive.

After 1894 the importation of laborers was conducted by Japanese companies. The United States became involved when Japan sent a warship to settle a problem between a Japanese company and the Hawai'i government. For a while the United States considered annexing Hawai'i. The problem was finally settled peacefully and the Hawai'i government agreed to pay the Japanese $75,000.

Annexation

In 1896, a Republican, William McKinley, was elected president of the United States. The country was now more sympathetic to annexation. However, it was not the problem with Japan that finally caused Congress to favor annexation. It was the outbreak of the Spanish-American War on April 25, 1898. The war began with the sinking of the battleship *Maine* in the harbor at Havana, Cuba. American troops also went to the Philippines. Since no battleship at that time could steam from San Francisco to Manila without stopping midway, the United States realized how much it needed Hawai'i.

In 1897, Lili'uokalani went to Washington to protest the annexation treaty, which was being considered in the U.S. Senate.

To help the cause of annexation, President and Mrs. Dole made a trip to Washington early in 1898. However, many powerful interests in the United States worked against annexation. The sugar interests, represented by such men as Claus Spreckels, fought it. The Democratic Party also fought it.

More than half of American senators were in favor of annexation. To approve the annexation treaty, two-thirds of the senators needed to vote for it. Therefore, those in favor of annexation asked for a joint resolution. This required only a simple majority of both houses of Congress. This method had been used to annex Texas. By July 6, 1898, both houses of Congress approved annexation. The next day President McKinley signed the bill.

The news of annexation reached Honolulu on July 13, 1898. Fire bells rang, factory whistles blew, firecrackers exploded, and the artillery in front of the Executive Building boomed out a 100-gun salute. The crowd that had gathered at the waterfront

Annexation announcement in the *Pacific Commercial Advertiser*, July 14, 1898. Hawai'i State Archives

to hear President Dole read the news marched uptown with the band. That evening a group of citizens lit a huge bonfire at the foot of Punchbowl.

The official ceremony did not take place until August 12, 1898. The flag that Minister Blount had ordered lowered in 1893 was once more raised over the Hawaiian Islands.

On August 12, 1898, the Hawaiian flag was lowered at the Executive Building ('Iolani Palace) and replaced with the American flag. Hawai'i State Archives

Sanford B. Dole turned over control of the former Republic of Hawai'i to the United States in the annexation ceremony of August 12, 1898.
Hawai'i State Archives

Americans, Portuguese, Chinese, and Japanese attended the annexation ceremonies—but no Hawaiians.

The Islands were officially a part of the United States, but until the passage of the Organic Act in 1900, they continued under the laws of the republic. The same officials remained in office for another two years.

Lili'uokalani's Final Years

After Lili'uokalani's imprisonment ended, she returned to Washington Place. In 1897 she wrote *Hawaii's Story by Hawaii's Queen.* In 1909 she set up a fund to help Hawaiian children. Today the Queen Lili'uokalani Children's Center helps over two thousand children a year.

Lili'uokalani died on November 11, 1917. She is buried in the Royal Mausoleum in Nu'uanu.

Queen Lili'uokalani in 1900. Hawai'i State Archives

Summing Up the Chapter

Trouble faced Lili'uokalani, Hawai'i's only reigning queen, almost as soon as she came to the throne. The country was in the middle of an economic depression. The struggle for political power continued. The two main issues—control of the cabinet and changing the constitution—finally led to the overthrow of the monarchy. The Annexation Club wanted to do away with the monarchy, set up a provisional government, and ask to be annexed to the United States. Those who were against annexation pledged loyalty to the queen and supported her plan to change the constitution only by legal means. The annexationists formed a Committee of Public Safety and asked the United States minister to land sailors and marines to help keep order.

A provisional government was formed, headed by Sanford Dole. The overthrow of the government was peaceful.

Lili'uokalani is seated between Sanford B. Dole, left, and Governor Lucius Pinkham, right, at a birthday celebration for bandleader Henry Berger, standing, in 1914. Hawai'i State Archives

Lili'uokalani's signature.
Hawai'i State Archives

Lili'uokalani gave up her throne under protest. She believed that the actions of the American minister would not be supported by the United States. Representatives of the queen and those of the new provisional government went to the United States to plead their cause. Opinion in America was divided. President Cleveland studied the matter for some time and decided against any action. On July 4, 1894, a new constitution for the Republic of Hawai'i went into effect. Attempts by supporters of the queen to overthrow the republic failed.

A change in the United States tariff brought prosperity again to the sugar planters and a need to import workers from abroad. With the coming to office of President McKinley and the outbreak of the Spanish-American War, the question of annexation again arose. By joint resolution of the Senate and the House of Representatives, annexation was approved. The ceremonies on August 12, 1898, were attended by peoples of many nationalities but not by Hawaiians.

Appendixes

APPENDIX A   Location and Formation of the Hawaiian Islands

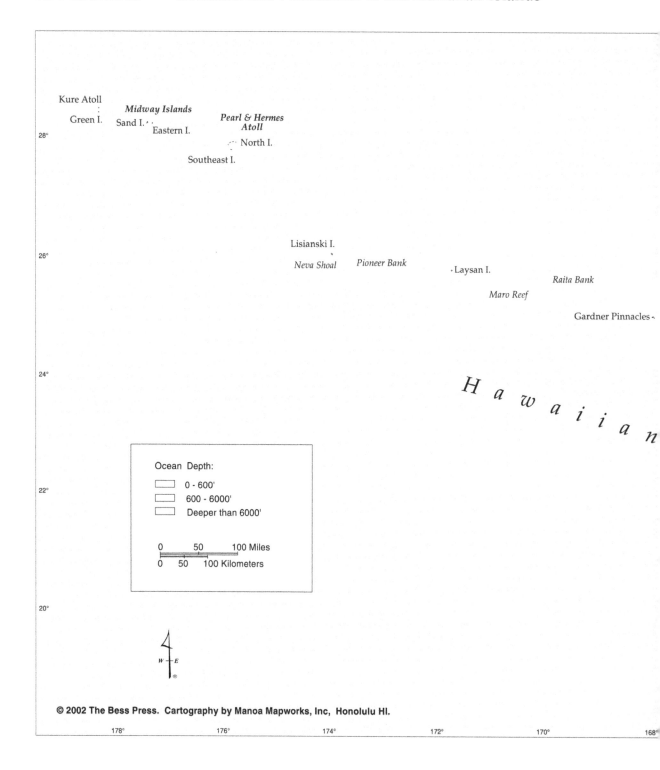

Kure Atoll

Green I.

Midway Islands

Sand I.

Eastern I.

Pearl & Hermes Atoll

North I.

Southeast I.

28°

26°

Lisianski I.

Neva Shoal   *Pioneer Bank*

Laysan I.

Raita Bank

Maro Reef

Gardner Pinnacles

24°

Ocean Depth:

0 - 600'

600 - 6000'

Deeper than 6000'

0   50   100 Miles

0   50   100 Kilometers

22°

20°

W — E

© 2002 The Bess Press. Cartography by Manoa Mapworks, Inc, Honolulu HI.

178°   176°   174°   172°   170°   168°

The Hawaiian Islands consist of many islands, reefs, and shoals strung out in the Pacific Ocean for 1,600 miles, about the same distance as that from St. Louis, Missouri, to Seattle, Washington.

THE HAWAIIAN
ISLANDS

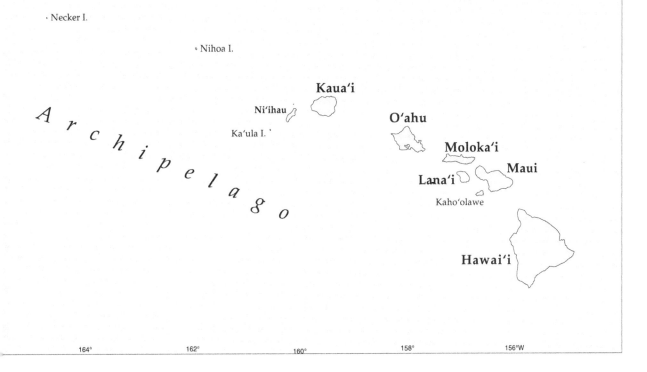

North Pacific Ocean

· Necker I.

◦ Nihoa I.

Kaua'i

Ni'ihau

O'ahu

Ka'ula I. ˙

Moloka'i

Lana'i   **Maui**

Kaho'olawe

A r c h i p e l a g o

Hawai'i

164°   162°   160°   158°   156°W

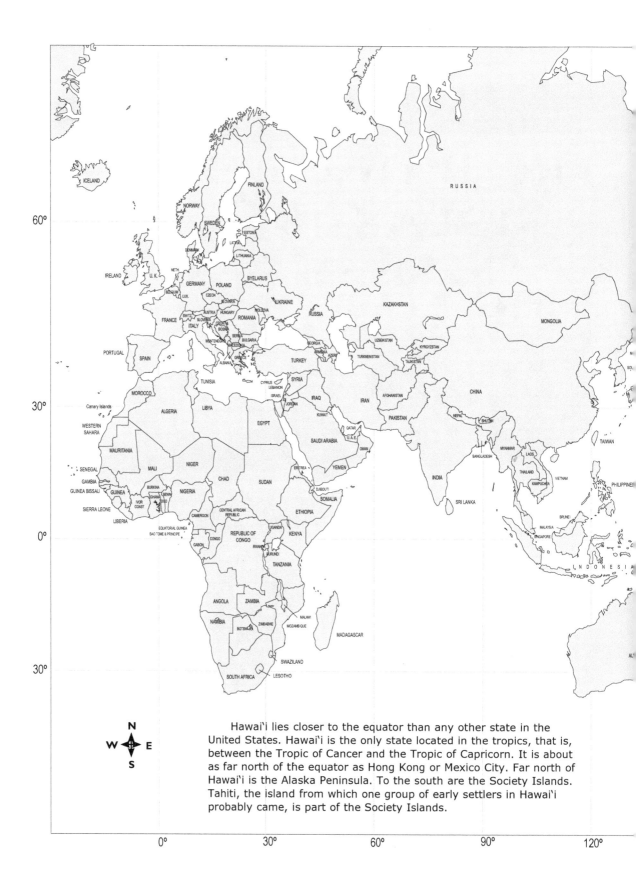

Hawai'i lies closer to the equator than any other state in the United States. Hawai'i is the only state located in the tropics, that is, between the Tropic of Cancer and the Tropic of Capricorn. It is about as far north of the equator as Hong Kong or Mexico City. Far north of Hawai'i is the Alaska Peninsula. To the south are the Society Islands. Tahiti, the island from which one group of early settlers in Hawai'i probably came, is part of the Society Islands.

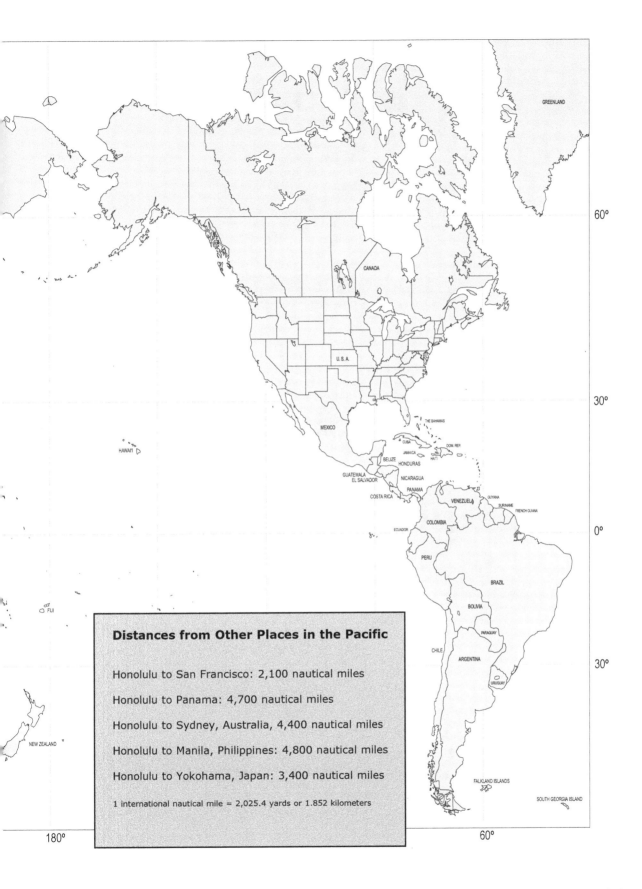

Distances from Other Places in the Pacific

Honolulu to San Francisco: 2,100 nautical miles

Honolulu to Panama: 4,700 nautical miles

Honolulu to Sydney, Australia, 4,400 nautical miles

Honolulu to Manila, Philippines: 4,800 nautical miles

Honolulu to Yokohama, Japan: 3,400 nautical miles

1 international nautical mile = 2,025.4 yards or 1.852 kilometers

Formation of the Islands

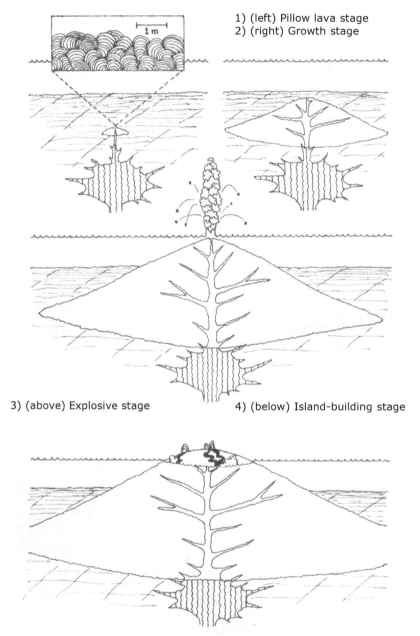

1) (left) Pillow lava stage
2) (right) Growth stage

1 m

3) (above) Explosive stage

4) (below) Island-building stage

Diagram by Lyn Lawrence

One or a few large volcanoes built each of the major islands. Quiet eruptions of melted rock built great piles of lava rock that grew up through the ocean. Melted rock oozed out in long, tube-shaped fingers. Their skin was cooled by the water to a glassy crust, but their insides were still liquid. At the ends of these fingers, bulbs of lava about the size of a trash barrel punched out and rolled away. Then they spread from their own weight to a pillow-like shape. A great pile of these pillow lavas is the base of every Hawaiian island.

As this great undersea mountain neared the ocean surface, eruptions became violent. Shallow water could not hold steam released when the hot lava boiled the seawater. Later, when the mountain grew high enough to wall out the sea, lava came from the earth by fountaining or by gently streaming from cracks and vents. From these eruptions long lava flows wind down even today.

The Earth's Moving Plates

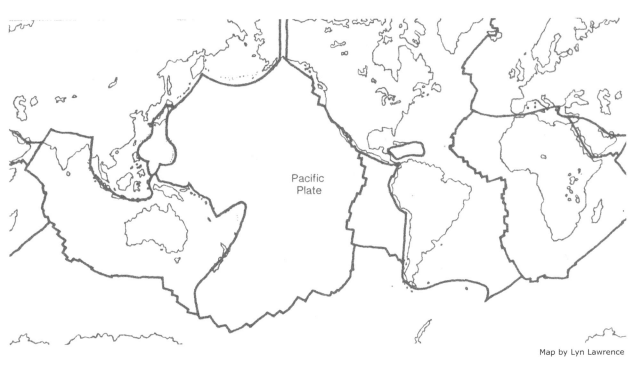

Pacific
Plate

Map by Lyn Lawrence

The crust of the Earth is a rocky skin, thinner in relation to the whole planet than the skin of an apple is to the whole fruit. The crust is broken into more than a dozen rigid plates. Where these plates meet along their edges, the major mountain ranges, oceanic deeps, volcanoes, and earthquakes appear.

The Hawaiian volcanoes, unlike most others, occur in the middle of a plate. Geologists are puzzled by this. They have tried to explain the chain of Hawaiian islands by thinking of a hot spot now beneath the island of Hawai'i, but before under each more westerly island in turn. In this theory, the hot spot stays in place, pushing magma up to build each island as the Pacific Plate moves slowly westward. A chain of islands thus trails out from the hot spot, with the older islands toward the west. The plate moves only a few inches a year, but this motion has gone on for many millions of years.

The Stages of Island Growth

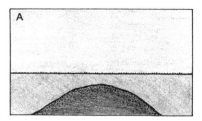

Lava builds a mountain under the sea.

Lava builds a dome island.

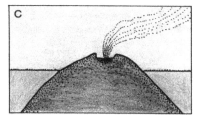

A caldera forms at the top of the dome.

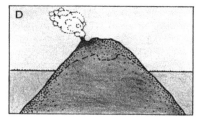

Sometimes the caldera is covered by a cap of lava. Cones form on the sides.

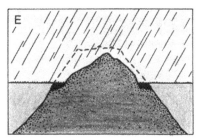

The sea and rain wear down the island. Coral starts to grow.

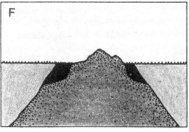

The sea is lower, then higher again. When it is higher, much more coral grows. The island sinks some more.

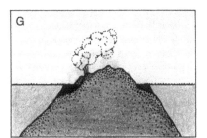

The sea is lower again. Small cones send out lava. Reefs are made. The island settles some more.

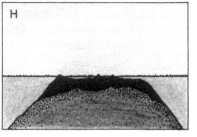

The island settles under the sea. Only reefs are left. The island has become an atoll.

Diagram by Lyn Lawrence

Much of the shoreline of the islands contains reefs. These reefs extend out into the water from 1/2 mile to 3 1/2 miles. They have a rough, uneven surface.

Very small animals called "polyps" generally build coral reefs. These polyps live in colonies under just the right conditions of water temperature and salt content. Each new generation attaches its shell to the shells of its ancestors. It is this process of building their homes, one on top of the other, that forms a reef. Other coral marine life, such as algae, make their homes in the shells of the polyps, filling much of the empty space. In time the reef becomes solid limestone.

When a main island-building volcano becomes extinct, slow erosion and sinking gradually bring the mountain down to sea level. As sinking continues, the volcanic rock disappears as it is buried under growing coral reefs. Reef plants and animals build new limestone layers to maintain the islands even as they keep sinking. The resulting coral atolls often form rings reaching only a few feet above sea level, making shallow lagoons. Later changes in sea level and plate movement of the islands into cooler northerly waters kill the reef organisms. The islands then sink beneath the sea, never to be seen again.

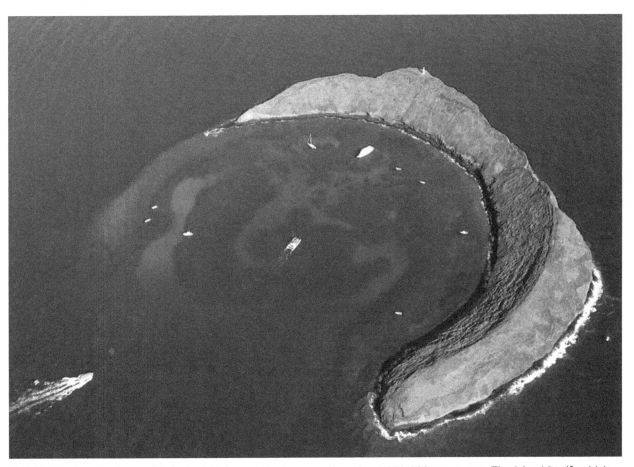

Molokini Crater, offshore of Haleakalā Volcano, Maui, was active about 230,000 years ago. The island itself, which rises only 49 meters (162 feet) above sea level, is a bird sanctuary, off-limits to visitors, but snorkelers and divers can enjoy the abundant marine life in and around the crater. © 1994 Aris Multimedia Entertainment, Inc. © (P) John Forte

APPENDIX B   Geography of the Islands

The Northwestern Hawaiian Islands

Size: 3 square miles

Population: 5

Geology: Nihoa, Necker, French Frigate Shoals, and Gardner Pinnacles are what is left of heavily eroded shield volcanoes; Maro Reef, Laysan, Lisianski, Pearl and Hermes Atoll, Midway Islands, and Kure Atoll are limestone islands.

Unique features: Important in the study of island and coral reef ecology; all the islands except Midway Islands and Kure Atoll are part of the Hawaiian Islands National Wildlife Refuge.

Two adult brown noddies from Lisianski Island grooming each other. Maia Yannacone

Kaua'i

Size: 552 square miles

Population: 58,303

Geology: oldest of the main islands; formed from a single shield volcano

Economy: tourism, taro, coffee, sugar

Unique features: Wai'ale'ale may have the highest annual rainfall in the world, 485 inches; damaged by Hurricane Iwa in 1982 and Hurricane 'Iniki in 1992.

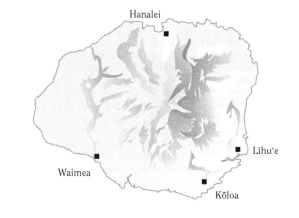

Waimea Canyon, Kaua'i. © 1994 Aris Multimedia Entertainment, Inc. © (P) John Forte

Kalalau, Kaua'i. © 1994 Aris Multimedia Entertainment, Inc. © (P) John Forte

Ni'ihau

Size: 69 square miles

Population: 160

Geology: formed from a single shield volcano

Economy: ranching

Unique features: privately owned by the Robinson family; limited visitor access; Halulu Lake is the largest natural lake in the Hawaiian Islands (182 acres); residents make prized Ni'ihau shell leis.

O'ahu

Size: 596 square miles

Population: 876,151

Geology: four geologic regions: the Wai'anae Range, the Ko'olau Range, the Schofield Plateau, and the coastal plain, made up of elevated coral reef

Economy: tourism, government services (including the military)

Unique features: Diamond Head, a tuff cone (landform created by an explosive eruption)

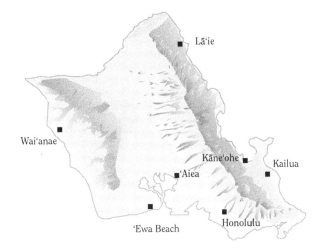

Diamond Head, O'ahu. © 1994 Aris Multimedia Entertainment, Inc. © (P) John Forte

Waikīkī Beach, O'ahu. © 1994 Aris Multimedia Entertainment, Inc. © (P) John Forte

Molokaʻi

Size: 260 square miles

Population: 7,404

Geology: formed by two large and one small shield volcanoes

Economy: tourism, diversified agriculture, cattle raising

Unique features: Kalaupapa, the Hansen's disease settlement

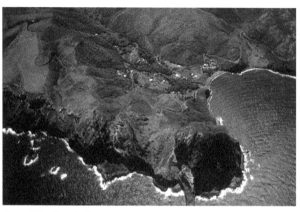

Onealiʻi, Molokaʻi. © 1994 Aris Multimedia Entertainment, Inc. © (P) John Forte

Garden of the Gods, Lānaʻi.
© 1994 Aris Multimedia Entertainment, Inc. © (P) John Forte

Lānaʻi

Size: 141 square miles

Population: 3,193

Geology: formed from a single shield volcano

Economy: tourism

Unique features: Formerly a large pineapple plantation, the island is now privately owned; Garden of the Gods, a lava flow region with unusual rock formations

Kahoʻolawe

Size: 44 square miles

Population: uninhabited (pre-1800 population of about 200)

Geology: the summit of a volcanic dome

Unique features: From 1941–1990 was used by U.S. military as an artillery range; in 1981 was Placed on National Register of Historic Places; in 1994 was returned to State of Hawaiʻi.

Maui

Size: 727 square miles

Population: 117, 644

Geology: formed by two volcanoes, West Maui and Haleakalā

Economy: tourism, sugar, pineapple, diversified agriculture (onions, potatoes, fruits, flowers), cattle ranching

Unique features: ʻIao Needle, a 2,250-foot-tall natural landform

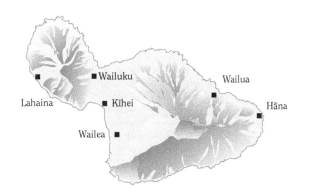

ʻIao Needle, Maui. © 1994 Aris Multimedia Entertainment, Inc. © (P) John Forte

Kīlauea Crater, Hawaiʻi. © 1994 Aris Multimedia Entertainment, Inc. © (P) John Forte

Hawaiʻi

Size: largest; 4,028 square miles

Population: 148,677

Geology: formed by five volcanoes: Mauna Kea, Mauna Loa, Hualālai, Kohala, Kīlauea

Economy: diversified agriculture (papaya, flowers, Kona coffee, macadamia nuts), ranching, and tourism (Kona coast and Hawaiʻi Volcanoes National Park)

Unique features: Mauna Loa and Kīlauea are the only two active volcanoes in the state; Mauna Kea is the world's tallest mountain, from ocean floor to peak; subject to more natural hazards (volcanic eruptions, earthquakes, tsunamis, flooding, drought) than any of the other islands.

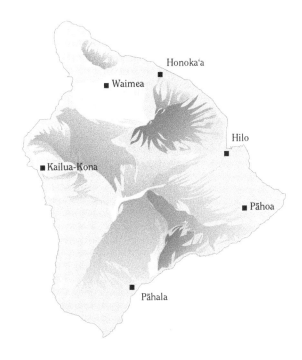

Hawai'i's Climate

A Lāna'i beach. © 1994 Aris Multimedia Entertainment, Inc. © (P) John Forte

Hawai'i's climate is subtropical, with steady northwest trade winds. The average temperature for the state is 72 degrees, with a daily temperature range of 10 degrees.

Waterfall on the way to Hāna, Maui.
© 1994 Aris Multimedia Entertainment, Inc. © (P) John Forte

The northeast, or windward, sides of islands receive large amounts of rainfall.

Oneali'i, Moloka'i. © 1994 Aris Multimedia Entertainment, Inc. © (P) John Forte

The leeward sides (south and west, facing away from the trade winds) of the islands are usually dry, except during so-called "Kona" weather, when the trade winds stop blowing and the winds come from the south. This type of weather brings uncomfortably hot and humid weather to most of the island and rain to the leeward side.

Mauna Kea, Hawai'i. B. Bess

For every 1,000 feet of increase in altitude the temperature drops about 3 degrees. Because the tops of Mauna Loa and Mauna Kea are above the trade winds, they get little rain, but may have snow during the winter.

APPENDIX C   Origins and Migrations of the Polynesians

Many centuries ago the ancestors of the Polynesian peoples came into an area known today as Oceania. It is made up of more than ten thousand islands, which modern geographers divided into three parts: Melanesia, Micronesia, and Polynesia. It is thought that these people journeyed slowly from Southeast Asia, through the islands of Indonesia, and from there to the far-flung islands of the Pacific.

Settlement of Oceania

During the last Ice Age (15,000 to 20,000 years ago) the ocean level was 150 to 350 feet lower than it is today. Many areas now under water were once dry land. Over this land bridge from Asia came the ancestors of the native peoples of Australia, New Guinea, and parts of Melanesia. They migrated not all at once but over a period of many centuries. Since distances between the land masses were short, these people needed only very simple boats for travel and probably were seldom out of sight of land.

Centuries later, other tribal and family groups sailed farther eastward. They settled the rest of Melanesia and the islands of Micronesia and Polynesia. These explorations took place many centuries before the great Western European voyages.

Settlement of Polynesia

By slow stages the islands of western Polynesia were discovered and simple communities founded. Centers of culture were formed in Samoa and the Society Islands in southeastern Polynesia. Further daring expeditions

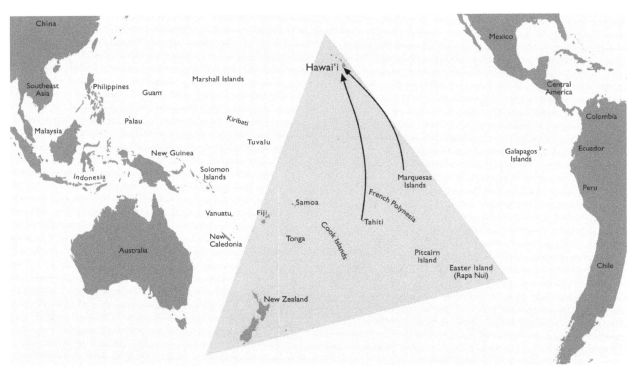

The darker blue area is the "Polynesian Triangle." The arrows show paths of migration to Hawai'i from the Marquesas (A.D. 300–600) and from Tahiti (A.D. 1000–1300).

would follow, toward New Zealand to the south, Hawai'i to the north, and Easter Island to the East—the great "Polynesian Triangle."

The Hawaiian Islands were among the last to be discovered by the Polynesians. In the past, scholars believed that Hawai'i was first settled by Tahitians about 1000 A.D. However, archeologists have uncovered evidence that the first Hawaiians came from the Marquesas at least 500 years earlier. Because Hawaiian culture is so closely related to Tahitian culture, there is reason to believe that, although the first settlers came from the Marquesas, the later ones were from Tahiti.

How the Polynesians Crossed the Great Ocean

In what kinds of boats did the Polynesians make their amazing journeys? Long before sailors of the Mediterranean and the Atlantic dared to venture far from land, Polynesian canoes were crossing and recrossing the 2,400 miles between Hawai'i and Tahiti. From the central Pacific they sailed eastward to discover Rapa Nui (Easter Island), a distance of 2,500 miles with no in-between stopping places.

For ordinary fishing and travel to nearby islands, the Polynesians used a simple canoe hollowed out of logs with the aid of stone adzes. Usually these canoes were small, although some were more than fifty feet long. A more stable craft was the outrigger canoe, made by attaching a floating *ama*, or outrigger, to a single canoe. The *ama* is a pole of light wood, fastened to the hull by two crosspieces extending outward from the hull. It rests on the surface of the water and helps to keep the canoe from tipping. With the *ama*, small vessels could be used for fairly long journeys even in rough water.

For long voyages, two canoes were joined together by wooden crossties or by a platform pulled between them. The large twin canoes had

A Polynesian double canoe. Painting by © Herb Kawainui Kāne

one or two masts set in this platform. Often a deck house thatched with pandanus leaves was built on the platform for shelter from the sun and rain.

When the Europeans arrived in Polynesia, they found the islanders using Tongan single canoes, which could be 150 feet long. A triangular sail was hung by the middle of one side from the mast, which was fastened to the deck or the front of the canoe. The sail, not the canoe, was reversed when the crew wished to change direction.

Preparations for the Voyage

When the Polynesians set out on a long voyage to a new home, they planned very carefully. First they inspected their canoes for any weaknesses. Everything had to be in perfect order for the coming battle with the mighty ocean. Then they stocked the canoe with food and water. Since their new island home might have few natural resources, they took with them seeds and food plants, pigs, dogs, and fowl.

The foods for the voyage were usually cooked. Voyagers starting from atolls took ripe pandanus fruit grated into a coarse flour, cooked, dried, and packed into bundles protected by an outer wrapping of dried pandanus leaves. The voyagers starting from volcanic islands took preserved breadfruit carried in fairly large baskets and sweet potatoes that had been cooked and dried. Also onboard was dried shellfish, which could be kept indefinitely. Fowls were cooped in canoes, fed with dried coconut meat, and killed and eaten when necessary. Master fishermen caught deep-sea fish, including sharks. Food could be cooked over a fireplace laid on a bed of sand on the deck. Fresh water was carried in coconut water jugs, gourds, or lengths of bamboo.

After waiting for the right season of the year, they decided on the perfect day to set forth. When all the omens were favorable and the gods had been honored, they raised their mat sails, passed through the reefs, and steered for the horizon.

The Crossing

They had no compass or log book. They guided themselves by the sun and the stars, by the flight of the birds, by cloud formations, and by the actions of the waves and winds. Polynesian navigators knew and could name 150 or more stars. They kept track of the days by tying knots in a piece of string.

Year after year these daring voyagers piloted their double canoes across the waters of the Pacific. One by one the islands of the Pacific were discovered. Some were dry and not fit for settlement. Others were green and could support life. Among the most livable of these were what are now known as the Hawaiian Islands.

When the ancient Polynesians arrived in the Hawaiian Islands, they brought with them their old ways of doing things. Later, they changed them to fit the conditions of their new home. And then suddenly, for some reason still unknown, the period of the "long voyages" ended. The people who had reached Hawai'i lived apart from the rest of the world. In this period, lasting centuries, they developed their own culture.

After some centuries the Islands were discovered again, this time by Europeans and Americans, who brought a new god and new ways.

Glossary

abode: a place to live in.

abolished: gotten rid of.

administrator: someone who manages people and events.

adobe: bricks made of clay and straw.

ali'i: chiefs.

ambitious: wanting to have more money or power.

amnesty: pardon; forgiveness, with no threat of punishment.

annexation: adding another area of land or political unit to one's own.

antagonist: an opponent, enemy.

ap: a term that in Welsh names means "son of."

appease: to calm.

arable: fit for crops to grow in.

arrowroot: a plant whose root is used to make a starch for food.

artillerymen: soldiers trained in the use of weapons.

bartered: traded.

blockade: an action preventing ships from entering or leaving a harbor.

boatswain: a low-ranking ship's officer in charge of the rigging, anchors, cables, and deck crew.

boom: a period of growth.

brig: a two-masted, square-sailed ship.

Burma: a Southeast Asian country known today as Myanmar.

capital: money that can be used to make more money.

census: an official count of the population.

cession: the giving up of control to someone else.

chronometer: an extremely accurate clock that can be used to determine longitude.

circular: a notice given out to large numbers of people.

civil war: fighting between groups or regions within the same country.

colonies: areas controlled by a far-off country.

commoners: the people who did not have the rank of chiefs; in Hawai'i they were known as the *maka'āinana*.

confederation: a group of countries joined together for a common purpose.

confidant: someone with whom private thoughts can be shared.

Congregational Church: a Protestant group in which each separate church governs itself.

conspiracy: an agreement between two or more people to do something criminal or illegal.

constitutional: based on a constitution, or written laws.

consul: a person who lives in a foreign country and looks after the interests of his or her country there.

converts: those who have adopted a belief.

coronation: a ceremony in which a king or queen is crowned and begins ruling.

crockery: pottery made from clay fired at fairly low temperatures.

daggers: short, pointed weapons with sharp edges.

descendants: those who come after; children, grandchildren.

desertion: leaving one's job on a ship.

diplomat: a representative of one country who works directly with the government of another country.

disastrous: terrible; causing great destruction and unhappiness.

disbanded: broke up.

dismantled: tore apart.

distilleries: places for making alcoholic beverages.

duty: a tax on imported goods.

encumbered: held back; slowed down.

epidemics: diseases spreading rapidly and infecting many people at one time.

episode: an event that is one of a series of related events.

excelling: doing especially well.

excommunicated: not allowed to remain a member of a church.

exhausting: very tiring.

exhibition: show.

expansion: growing larger by adding new land.

expel: throw out; remove by force.

exploited: made use of selfishly.

extricating: freeing.

factors: businesses that are paid to perform services for other businesses.

felicity: pleasantness of sound or style.

fermented: changed by yeast from sugar and carbon dioxide to alcohol.

feuds: disagreements that last for a long period.

fluently: smoothly and easily.

fowl: a chicken or turkey.

frigate: a high-speed, medium-sized sailing warship.

genealogies: family trees, showing the descent of families from their ancestors; family histories.

genealogists: people who study family histories.

grazier: a person who raises cattle.

Guayaquil: a city in western Ecuador.

hānai: adoption.

haole: foreigners.

haven: a safe place.

heathen: not a member of an established religion.

heiau: a temple.

hereditary: passed from one family member to another.

hūnākele: "to hide in secret."

immunity: protection or resistance.

infanticide: the killing of unwanted babies.

influence: power, control.

invalid: someone who suffers constantly from being ill or disabled.

job printing: small printing projects such as flyers and cards.

kāhuna: priests, experts.

kāhuna kuahau: historians.

kanaka: Hawaiian word for "person."

kapu: something that is not allowed.

kapu system: a set of rules telling Hawaiians what they could and could not do.

kīhei: a cape made of *kapa* (bark cloth), worn over one shoulder and tied in a knot.

konohiki: a headman of an *ahupua'a,* or land section.

kuhina nui: prime minister.

Kūkā'ilimoku: one of the forms of the god Kū; Kamehameha's family war god.

kukui: a tree whose oily nuts were used for lamps.

kuleana: responsibility, right, or ownership.

lenient: not harsh or strict.

leprosy: a somewhat contagious disease that causes loss of feeling.

limu: seaweed.

literacy: ability to read and write.

mahele: division.

maka'āinana: common people.

māmalahoe: splintered paddle.

Manila: a city in the Philippine Islands.

man-of-war: a warship.

martial law: law enforced by military forces.

monopoly: control by one group.

mortgaged: offered in payment for debts.

mutiny: open rebellion against a leader by his followers.

negotiate: to reach an agreement through discussion.

neutral: not taking either side.

New Hebrides: islands northeast of Australia known today as Vanuatu.

pāhoa: Hawaiian dagger.

palapala: printed matter.

Panic of 1819: an economic depression sometimes called "America's first great economic crisis."

paramount: of highest rank or power.

pardoned: forgiven; excused from punishment.

pā'ū: kapa (bark cloth) skirt.

pavilions: temporary tents set up for special events.

persecution: hurtful behavior toward a particular person or group.

pestilence: a usually fatal disease that affects many people at the same time.

pī'āpā: alphabet.

picul: a measure used for sandalwood. One picul equaled 133.5 pounds and was worth about 8 or 10 dollars.

plunder: to rob, especially during a war.

poi: food made from pounded and watered taro; it is sometimes made from breadfruit or sweet potato.

prelude: something that leads to something else.

price supports: money paid to farmers to make market prices for crops equal to what farmers expect to get.

primers: elementary textbooks for teaching children to read.

privateers: privately owned ships that were allowed during wartime to attack and capture enemy ships.

privy council : a group of advisors to the king.

procession: a group moving in an orderly, formal manner.

proclamations: official public announcements.

promissory notes: written promises to repay a certain amount at a certain time.

prosper: become richer or more successful.

protectorate: a country or region under the protection and partial control of a stronger country.

provisional: for the time being, temporary.

provisioned: stocked with food and other supplies.

pulu: a silky or wooly fiber that grows at the base of tree fern fronds; it was used as a filling for mattresses and pillows.

quarantined: kept away from others to prevent the spread of disease.

reciprocity: an equal exchange; giving and getting the same thing in return.

recitation: saying something out loud, from memory, for an audience.

refit: restock and repair.

regent: someone who rules for someone else who is absent or too young.

remorse: sorrow and shame.

repeal: cancel.

republic: a government run by representatives elected by the people.

revolution: a complete change.

rivalry: competition.

rudiments: basic skills.

Sabbath: day of rest and worship.

salvaged: rescued, saved.

scandal: a shameful event that is made public.

scarcity: shortage.

schooner: a sailing vessel with at least two masts; the largest sail is on the aftermost mast.

scurvy: a disease caused by not getting enough vitamin C.

seminary: a school, usually for training ministers.

Siam: a Southeast Asian country known today as Thailand.

skirmish: a small or less important battle.

slaughter: the killing of a large number of people.

sloop: a sailing boat with a single mast.

successor: the person who follows after or replaces another in an office or position, such as king.

sundered: separated.

surveying: determining the boundaries of a piece of land.

tariffs: taxes on imported goods.

temperaments: personalities, characters.

tenants: those who pay to use or live on land owned by someone else.

thriving: successful.

tidepools: water that collects in rocky hollows at the shoreline at low tide.

title: legal ownership.

toiled: worked hard.

toleration: respect for the beliefs and acts of others.

traditional: passed down from generation to generation.

treacherous: not to be trusted.

treasonable: disloyal.

truck gardening: growing vegetables to sell.

uncouth: rough, uncivilized.

unification: bringing together into one unit.

vaccinate: to protect from disease by injecting with a very weak form of the disease bacteria or virus.

vandalism: purposeful destruction of public or private property.

vocational: work-related.

Bibliography

Recently published books:

Armstrong, William. *Around the World with a King.* Honolulu: Mutual Publishing, 1995. An account of Kalākaua's world tour.

Cachola, Jean Iwata. *Kamehameha III: Kauikeaouli.* Honolulu: Kamehameha Schools Press, 1995. An easy-to-read biography illustrated with photographs and line drawings.

Comeau, Rosalin Uphus. *Kamehameha V: Lot Kapuāiwa.* Honolulu: Kamehameha Schools Press, 1996. An easy-to-read biography illustrated with photographs and line drawings.

Desha, Stephen. Trans. by Frances N. Fisher. *Kamehameha and His Warrior Kekūhaupi'o.* Honolulu: Kamehameha Schools Press, 2000. The life story of a warrior who trained and fought alongside Kamehameha the Great.

Donohugh, Donald. *The Story of Kōloa: A Kaua'i Plantation.* Honolulu: Mutual Publishing, 2001.

Dunford, Betty, et al. *The Hawaiians of Old.* 3d ed. Honolulu: The Bess Press, 2002. The latest edition of a classic textbook, illustrated with paintings by Herb Kawainui Kāne.

Galuteria, Peter. *Lunalilo.* Rev. ed. Honolulu: Kamehameha Schools Press, 1993. An easy-to-read biography illustrated with photographs and line drawings.

Ii, John Papa. Ed. By Dorothy B. Barrère. *Fragments of Hawaiian History.* Honolulu: Bishop Museum Press, 1995.

Juvik, James O., Thomas R. Paradise, Sonia P. Juvik. *Student Atlas of Hawai'i.* Honolulu: The Bess Press, 2000. Colorful maps, charts, and photographs and clear text illustrate and explain the significance of Hawai'i's mid-Pacific location.

Kamakau, Samuel M. *Ruling Chiefs of Hawaii.* Rev. ed. Honolulu: Kamehameha Schools Press, 1992. Particularly interesting as an interpretation by a scholar of Hawaiian ancestry who lived close to some of the events he describes.

Kāne, Herb Kawainui. *Ancient Hawai'i.* Captain Cook, Hawai'i: The Kawainui Press, 1997.

Liliuokalani. *Hawaii's Story by Hawaii's Queen*: Honolulu: Mutual Publishing, 1994. An affecting autobiography that presents the Queen's view of events leading to the loss of her throne.

Lowe, Ruby Hasegawa. *David Kalākaua.* Honolulu: Kamehameha Schools Press, 1998. An illustrated, easy-to-read biography.

———. *Kamehameha IV: Alexander Liholiho.* Honolulu: Kamehameha Schools Press, 1997. An illustrated, easy-to-read biography.

———. *Lili'uokalani.* Honolulu: Kamehameha Schools Press, 1993. An illustrated, easy-to-read biography.

Osorio, Jonathan Kay Kamakawiwo'ole. *Dismembering Lāhui: A History of the Hawaiian Nation to 1887.* Honolulu: University of Hawai'i Press, 2002. A Native Hawaiian scholar describes the Hawaiian people's attempts to retain political control from 1840 to 1887.

Quanchi, Max. *Atlas of the Pacific Islands.* Honolulu: The Bess Press, 2003. Presents up-to-date and accurate coverage of Pacific islands and the world through detailed maps and high-interest case studies.

Rayson, Ann, and Helen Bauer. *Hawai'i: The Pacific State.* Honolulu: The Bess Press, 1997. A full-color, single-volume overview of Hawai'i, its history, geography, and people.

Stannard, David E. *Before the Horror: The Population of Hawai'i on the Eve of Western Contact.* Honolulu: Social Science Research Institute, University of Hawai'i, 1989. Documents the effect of Western diseases on the Hawaiian population.

Williams, Julie Stewart. *Kamehameha the Great.* Rev. ed. Honolulu: Kamehameha Schools Press, 1993. An illustrated, easy-to-read biography.

———. *Princess Bernice Pauahi Bishop.* Rev. ed. Honolulu: Kamehameha Schools Press, 1998. An illustrated, easy-to-read biography.

Williams, Julie Stewart, and Suelyn Ching Tune. *Kamehameha II: Liholiho and the Impact of Change.* Honolulu: Kamehameha Schools Press, 2002. An illustrated, easy-to-read biography.

Pre-1970 sources:

Books:

Alexander, Arthur C. *Koloa Plantation*, 1835–1935. *Honolulu: Star-Bulletin* Printing Company, 1937. A history of the oldest Hawaiian sugar plantation.

Alexander, Mary Charlotte, and Charlotte Peabody Dodge. *Punahou: 1841–1941.* Berkeley: University of California Press, 1941. An authoritative account of events and personalities in the long history of this private school in Honolulu.

Alexander, William De Witt. *A Brief History of the Hawaiian People.* New York: American Book Company, 1899. A standard concise history for younger readers that includes the story of Hawai'i to Annexation.

Anderson, Bern. *Surveyors of the Sea: The Life and Voyages of Captain George Vancouver.* Seattle: University of Washington Press, 1960. Contains two interesting chapters dealing with Vancouver's relations with Kamehameha I.

Bingham, Hiram. *A Residence of Twenty-One Years in the Sandwich Islands.* 2d. ed. New York: Sherman Converse, 1848. A basic work in Hawaiian history.

Byron, Lord George. *Voyage of HMS* Blonde *to the Sandwich Islands in the Years 1824–1825.* London: John Murray, 1826. A colorful description of the voyage compiled from various journals and notes of some of the officers who accompanied Lord Byron.

Campbell, Archibald. *A Voyage Around the World,* 1806–1812. Edinburgh: Constable, 1816. 4th ed. printed by Allen Watts, Roxbury, Massachusetts, 1825.

Castle and Cooke. *The First 100 Years.* Honolulu, 1951. A report on the operations of one of Hawai'i's most powerful firms for the years 1851 to 1951.

Charlot, Jean. *Choris and Kamehameha.* Honolulu: Bishop Museum Press, 1958.

Chinen, Jon T. *The Great Mahele: Hawaii's Land Division of 1848.* Honolulu: University of Hawai'i Press, 1958. A very short book with a useful bibliography.

Coan, Titus. *Life in Hawaii.* New York: D. F. Anson, 1882. A first-hand account of a hard-working missionary's activities, chiefly on the island of Hawai'i, beginning in 1835.

Damon, Ethel M. *Father Bond of Kohala: A Chronicle of Pioneer Life in Hawaii.* Honolulu: The Friend, 1927. A well-compiled and -illustrated record of a life of service.

Dibble, Sheldon. *A History of the Hawaiian Islands.* Honolulu: Thos. G. Thrum, 1919. Written between 1836 and 1843 by a missionary teacher at the Mission Seminary at Lahainaluna, Maui.

Ellis, William. *Journal of William Ellis: A Narrative of a Tour through Hawaii in 1823.* Honolulu: Hawaiian Gazette Co. Inc., 1917. A reprint of the edition of 1827, a fascinating journal by an English missionary who lived in Hawai'i for about two years.

Fornander, Abraham. *An Account of the Polynesian Race.* 3 vols. London: Trubner and Co., 1878–1885. Ancient history of the Hawaiian people to the time of Kamehameha I, by a circuit judge of the island of Maui.

Fuchs, Lawrence H. *Hawaii Pono: A Social History.* Honolulu: Harcourt, Brace and World, Inc., 1961. Reprint. Honolulu: The Bess Press, 1993. An interpretation of political and social changes in Hawai'i, with emphasis on the years since 1890.

Gould, Maurice M., and Kenneth Bressett. *Hawaiian Coins, Tokens, and Paper Money.* Racine, Wisconsin: Whitman Publishing Co., 1960.

Halford, Francis John. *Nine Doctors and God.* Honolulu: University of Hawai'i Press, 1954. Lively account of nine missionary doctors, covering the period from 1820 to the close of the century, written by a Honolulu physician.

Hobbs, Jean. *Hawaii, A Pageant of the Soil.* Stanford: Stanford University Press, 1935. An excellent survey of the peculiarities of land tenure in Hawai'i.

Jarves, James Jackson. *Scenes and Scenery in the Sandwich Islands*, 1837–1842. Boston: James Munroe and Company, 1844. Another of the older guidebooks about the Islands, a companion to the author's *History*.

Judd, Gerrit P. *Hawaii: An Informal History.* New York: Crowell-Collier Publishing Company, 1961. A very useful, compressed history in paperback edition.

Judd, Laura Fish. *Honolulu: Sketches of Life in the Hawaiian Islands* from 1828 to 1861, reprinted by the *Honolulu Star-Bulletin*, 1928. Personal recollections by a missionary wife, with a supplementary chapter by her son bringing the events down to 1880.

Kalakaua, David. *The Legends and Myths of Hawaii.* New York: Charles L. Webster and Co., 1888. This collection of fables and folklore by King Kalākaua has a comprehensive introduction by R. M. Daggett, U. S. Minister to the Hawaiian Islands, who also edited the book.

Kuykendall, Ralph S. *The Hawaiian Kingdom.* 3 vols. Honolulu: University of Hawai'i Press, 1953. An important work by a noted historian of Hawai'i.

Kuykendall, Ralph S., and A. Grove Day. *Hawaii: A History from Polynesian Kingdom to American Statehood.* Rev. ed. New York: Prentice Hall, Inc., 1961. A skillfully compressed history designed for the general reader.

Malo, David. *Hawaiian Antiquities.* Honolulu: Bishop Museum Press, 1951. Written by one of the best authorities on Hawaiian practices and genealogy.

Steegmuller, Francis. *The Two Lives of James Jackson Jarves.* New Haven: Yale University Press, 1951. A biography of an early historian of Hawai'i and editor of *The Polynesian.*

Stewart, C. S. *A Visit to the South Seas.* Vol. II. New York: John P. Haven, 1833. A U.S. Navy chaplain's narrative of a visit to the Sandwich Islands in 1829–1830.

Thrum, Thomas G. *Hawaiian Annual and Standard Guide.* Honolulu: *Star-Bulletin* Printing Company. Published in various formats yearly since 1875, now appearing under the title *All about Hawaii*, in paperback. Extremely valuable statistics and informative articles.

Twain, Mark. *Letters from Hawaii.* Ed. A. Grove Day. Honolulu: The University Press of Hawai'i, 1966.

Wist, Benjamin O. *A Century of Public Education in Hawaii, October 15, 1840, to October 15, 1940.* The Hawaii Educational Review, 1940. Provides a helpful background for an understanding of Hawai'i's school system.

Yzendoorn, Reginald. *History of the Catholic Mission in the Hawaiian Islands.* Honolulu: *Star-Bulletin* Printing Company, 1927. Father Yzendoorn, SS.CC., tells the story of the Catholic missionaries in the Islands, with interesting comments about their relations with the Protestants.

Articles:

One of the most valuable sources of material concerning the history of Hawai'i and the customs and manners of the Hawaiian people is the collection of Annual Reports and Papers of the Hawaiian Historical Society. Of particular interest are the following articles, which have appeared in these publications. Numbers refer to Annual Reports unless otherwise noted.

Adler, Jacob. "Claus Spreckels' Rise and Fall in Hawaii," 67:1958.

Alexander, W. D. "Early Improvements in Honolulu Harbor," 15:1907.

_____. "The Birth of Kamehameha I," 19:1912.

Allen, Riley H. "Hawaii's Pioneers in Journalism," 37:1928.

Billiam-Walker, Donald. "Money of Hawaii," 48:1939.

Blue, George V. "Early Relations Between Hawaii and the Northwest Coast," 33:1924.

Bradley, Harold W. "Thomas ap Catesby Jones and the Hawaiian Islands, 1826–1827," 39:1930.

Bryan, E. H., Jr. "The Contributions of Thomas G. Thrum to Hawaiian History and Ethnology," 41:1932.

Cartwright, Bruce. "The First Discovery of Honolulu Harbor," 31:1922.

_____. "The Money of Hawaii," 38:1929.

Castle, W. R. "Centennial Reminiscences," 28:1919.

Clark, T. Blake. "Honolulu's Streets," 20:1938 (papers).

Damon, Ethel. "From Manoa to Punahou," 49:1940.

Davies, Theo. H. "The last Hours of Liholiho and Kamamalu," 4:1896.

Emerson, N.B. "The Honolulu Fort," 8:1901.

_____. "Mamala-Hoa," 10:1903.

_____. "The Poetry of Hawaii," 11:1904.

Gould, James Warren. "The Filibuster of Walter Murray Gibson," 68:1959.

Henriques, Edgar. "Hawaiian Canoes," 34:1925.

Hobbs, Jean. "The Land Title in Hawaii," 40:1931.

Howay, F. W. "Captain Henry Barber of Barber's Point," 47:1938.

Hoyt, Helen P. "Hawaii's First English Newspaper and Its Editor," 63:1954.

_____. "Theater in Hawaii, 1778–1840," 69:1960.

Judd, A. Francis. "Lunalilo, the Sixth King of Hawaii," 44:1935.

Judd, Bernice. "Koloa: A Sketch of Its Development," 44:1935.

King, Samuel Wilder. "The Hawaiians as Navigators and Seamen," 34:1925.

Kuykendall, Ralph S. "American Interests and American Influence in Hawaii in 1842," 39:1930.

_____. "The Schooner *Missionary Packet*," 41:1932.

_____. "The Earliest Japanese Labor Immigration to Hawaii," 43:1934.

_____. "Constitutions of the Hawaiian Kingdom," 21:1940 (papers).

Lyman, R. A. "Recollections of Kamehameha V," 3:1895.

Morris, Penrose C. "How the Territory of Hawaii Grew and What Domain It Covers," 42:1933.

Smith, Emerson C. "The History of Musical Development in Hawaii," 64:1955.

Spaulding, Thomas M. "Early Years of the Hawaiian Legislature," 38: 1929.

_____. "The Adoption of the Hawaiian Alphabet," 17:1930 (papers).

Stokes, John F. G., "New Bases for Hawaiian Chronology," 41:1932

_____. "Nationality of John Young, a Chief of Hawaii," 47: 1938.

_____. "Hawaii's Discovery by Spaniards—Theories Traced and Refuted," 20:1938 (papers).

Taylor, Albert Pierce. "Liholiho: A Revised Estimate of His Character," 15:1928 (papers).

Westervelt, W.D. "Legendary Places in Honolulu," 18:1911.

_____. "The First Twenty Years of Education in the Hawaiian Islands," 19:1912.

_____. "Kamehameha's Method of Government," 30:1921.

_____. "The Passing of Kamehameha I," 31:1922.

Periodicals:

The Friend

The first issue of this monthly newspaper appeared in January 1843, under the title of *The Temperance Advocate*. The second number added the words "And Seamen's Friend." In 1845 it appeared simply as *The Friend*. Published irregularly from 1847 to 1954.

The Hawaiian

Edited by Julien D. Hayne from May 1895 to March 1896. A short-lived antimissionary, antiannexation publication.

The Hawaiian Spectator, conducted by "an Association of Gentlemen," Honolulu, 1838. Essays by missionaries and writers including Richard Armstrong, John Diell, Artemas Bishop, Samuel Whitney, and James J. Jarves.

The Honolulu Advertiser

The oldest paper in Hawai'i with an unbroken record down to the present. First issued in July 1856 as a weekly under the name of *Pacific Commercial Advertiser*, edited by Henry M. Whitney. In 1882 the *Advertiser* became a daily.

The Honolulu Star-Bulletin

The first daily to live on to the present, this paper resulted from a merger of the *Evening Bulletin* and the *Hawaiian Star*. It appeared as a daily on April 24, 1882, one week ahead of the *Advertiser*.

The Polynesian

First issued as a weekly in Honolulu on June 6, 1840, edited by James Jackson Jarves. Within its scope, claimed the editor, were articles on "education, history, natural, civil, and political, biographies, discoveries, voyages, agricultural intelligence, statistics, languages, and commercial information."

Index

Numbers in bold text indicate illustrations.

Printed in the USA
CPSIA information can be obtained
at www.ICGtesting.com
CBHW042237311023
1547CB00001B/1